THE 2015 RHYSLING ANTHOLOGY

Also available from the
Science Fiction Poetry Association

The 2014 Rhysling Anthology:
The Best Science Fiction, Fantasy, and Horror Poetry of 2013
Edited by Elizabeth R. McClellan

The 2013 Rhysling Anthology:
The Best Science Fiction, Fantasy, and Horror Poetry of 2012
Edited by John C. Mannone

The 2012 Rhysling Anthology:
The Best Science Fiction, Fantasy, and Horror Poetry of 2011
Edited by Lyn C. A. Gardner

The 2011 Rhysling Anthology:
The Best Science Fiction, Fantasy, and Horror Poetry of 2010
Edited by David Lunde

The Alchemy of Stars: Rhysling Award Winners Showcase
Edited by Roger Dutcher and Mike Allen

Order from the SFPA Bookstore
astore.amazon.com/sfpoetry-20

Proceeds from the sale of *Confessions: A Nightmare in Five Acts*
(Elektric Milk Bath Press, 2013) go to support SFPA.

Order from elektrikmilkbathpress.com/bookstore

THE 2015 RHYSLING ANTHOLOGY

THE BEST SCIENCE FICTION, FANTASY, AND HORROR POETRY OF 2014

SELECTED BY THE
SCIENCE FICTION
POETRY ASSOCIATION

EDITED BY

Rich Ristow

Editor and Rhysling Chair: Rich Ristow
Book Design: F.J. Bergmann
Publisher: Science Fiction Poetry Association
Published in cooperation with: Hadrosaur Productions
SFPA President: Bryan D. Dietrich

Cover image: Bob Freeman, occultdetective.com

Cataloging-in-Publication Data

The 2015 Rhysling Anthology: the best science fiction, fantasy, and horror poetry of 2014 / selected by the Science Fiction Poetry Association; edited by Rich Ristow.

        p. cm.
    Includes bibliographical references.
    ISBN 978-1-885093-80-6
    1. Poetry. 2. Science fiction poetry. 3. Fantasy poetry. 4. Horror poetry.
    I. Ristow, Rich

For more information about the
Science Fiction Poetry Association,
visit www.sfpoetry.com

ACKNOWLEDGMENTS

Agner, Mary Alexandra. "Worlds Apart," *Polu Texni*, March.

Aisling, Kythryne. "Nothing Writes to Disk," *Stone Telling* 11.

Ali, Saira. "Main Sequence," *Mythic Delirium*, July.

Allen, Mike. "Dearly Beloved," *Postscripts to Darkness* 5.

Arkenberg, Megan. "Six Things the Owl Said," *Goblin Fruit*, Spring.

Barber, David. "The Delusion of Trees," *Eye to the Telescope* 14.

Barber, David. "Pauli Neutrino Telescope, Antarctica, July 14, 2033," *Star*Line* 37.2.

Bergmann, F.J. "Lost," *Eye to the Telescope* 14.

Bergmann, F.J. "100 Reasons to Have Sex with an Alien," 2014 SFPA Poetry Contest.

Berman, Ruth. "Science Fiction (with apologies to Marianne Moore's 'Poetry')," *Dreams and Nightmares* 98.

Betts, Matt. "Maybe Waldo Had Syphilis," *Tigershark* 5.

Borski, Robert. "The Cuckoo's Bride," *Dreams and Nightmares* 97.

Borski, Robert. "Sea Monster Objects to Term 'Kaiju'," *Dreams and Nightmares* 99.

Boston, Bruce. "Death of the Crossing Guard," *Jamais Vu* 1.

Boston, Bruce. "Septuagenarian Flashback," *Silver Blade* 24

Bradley, Lisa M. "Una Canción de Keys," *Strange Horizons*, 2/24/14.

Breiding, G. Sutton. "There Are Signs of Faerie Everywhere," facebook.com/gsuttonbreiding 7/5/14.

Cabeen, Robert Payne. "Rule 44," *Fearworms: Selected Poems* (Fanboy Comics).

Canfield, Michael. "Stalking a Wizard," *The Pedestal Magazine* 74.

Cato, Beth. "Dragon to Centauri," *Space & Time Magazine* 121.

Clark, G.O. "A Work in Progress," *Asimov's Science Fiction*, June.

Clink, David. "The Perfect Library," *If the World Were to Stop Spinning* (Piquant Press).

Clink, David. "Short Forms," *Asimov's Science Fiction*, September.

Cooney, C.S.E. "And I'll Dance With You Yet, My Darling," *Stone Telling* 10.

Cottier, P.S. "After hours in the op shop," *Eureka Street* 24:10.

Cox, Cardinal. "Keziah (Nahab) Mason," *Codex Lilith* (pamphlet).

Craven, Tim. "Neuroanatomy Practical," *Moon City Review* 2014.

Dietrich, Bryan D. "Drawn to Marvel," *Drawn to Marvel*, eds. Marta Ferguson & Bryan Dietrich (Minor Arcana Press).

Dietrich, Bryan D. "I Imagine My Mother's Death," *The Pedestal Magazine* 74.

Dietrich, Bryan D. "Stephen Hawking" *The Cresset* LXXIX:2.

Dorr, James S. "Beware of the Dog," *Grievous Angel*, 9/11/14.

Duthie, Peg. "Spelling 'For Worse'," *Goblin Fruit*, Winter.

Esaias, Timons. "A Universe," *Polu Texni*, May.

Evans, Kendall. "Star Song," *Analog*, July/August.

Forrest, Francesca. "The Peal Divers," *Strange Horizons*, 3/17/14.

Fusek, Serena. "House of Jaguar," *Star*Line* 37.4.

Gage, Joshua. "Extinction," *Star*Line* 37.3.

Gardner, Adele. "Row Your Boat Ashore," *Songs of Eretz Poetry E-zine* 2:2.

Gardner, Delbert R. "Hollow Beats the Night," *Songs of Eretz Poetry E-zine* 2:1.

Garey, Terry A. "Elephants in the Alley," *Cascadia Subduction Zone* 3:3.

Garfinkle, Gwynne. "It's a Universal Picture," *Mythic Delirium* 1.1.

Graham, Neile. "The Alchemy," *Goblin Fruit*, Winter.

Grant, April. "Roman Shade," *Strange Horizons*, 1/27/14.

Grey, John. "Mining Planet," *Chrome Baby*, Bairn 19.

Haskins, Lola. "Field Notes," *Analog*, November.

irving. "Before You Were a Vampire," *Star*Line* 37.3.

Johnson, John Philip. "After the Changeling Incantation," *Strange Horizons*, 2/3/14.

Kauderer, Herb. "After 'Dark Matter'," "After 'Signs You're in Trouble'," "Saline to Atlantis," "Words Not Red," *The Book of Answers* (Written Image).

Kindred, Sally Rosen. "Said Rapunzel to the Wolf," *Goblin Fruit*, Winter.

Kopaska-Merkel, David C. "Heere ther be Gods," *Star*Line* 37.4.

Kopaska-Merkel, David C. & W. Gregory Stewart. "Encounter While Waiting for Transport," *New Myths* 26.

Lee, Mary Soon. "Numbers," *Star*Line* 37.2.

Lee, Mary Soon. "The Matter of the Horses," *Ideomancer* 13:4.

Lee, Mary Soon. "The Virgin and the Unicorn," *Star*Line* 37.1.

Leibowitz, Sandi. "Attic Dust," *Silver Blade* 21.

Leibowitz, Sandi. "Braiding," *Niteblade* 27.

Lemberg, Rose. "Dualities," *Mythic Delirium*, October.

Lemberg, Rose. "Landwork," *Goblin Fruit*, Spring.

Lindow, Sandra J. "Cinderella Breast," *Archaeopteryx: The Newman Journal of Ideas* 2.

Lindow, Sandra J. "The Santa Claus Triptych," *Star*Line* 37.1.

Mannone, John C. "Butterfly Effect," *Tupelo Press 30/30 Project*.

Manzetti, Alessandro. "The Man Who Saw the World," *Venus Intervention* (Kipple Officina Libraria).

Marr, Jack Hollis. "A Summoning of Monsters," *Liminality* 1.

McBride, Lauren. "daydreaming," *Star*Line* 37.3.

McClellan, Elizabeth R. "Common Language," *2014 SFPA Poetry Contest*.

McClellan, Elizabeth R. "Concerning the Curious Burial Customs of the Witches of Megaira," *Interfictions* 4.

Mejía, Lynette. "The Time of Last Scattering," *Star*Line* 37.1.

Miller, P. Andrew. "Marvel Word Problems," *Drawn to Marvel*, eds. Marta Ferguson & Bryan Dietrich (Minor Arcana Press).

Neidigh, Kim L. "Odyssey," *Outposts of Beyond*, July.

Ness, Mari. "Demands," *Goblin Fruit*, Fall.

Odasso, A.J. "Queen of Cups," *inkscrawl* 7.

Odasso, A.J. & Dominik Parisien. "The Memory-Thief," *Ideomancer* 13:2.

Ogden, Aimee. "Morning Sickness," *Asimov's Science Fiction*, Oct/Nov.

Petrie, Simon. "At the Dark Matter Zoo," *The Stars Like Sand: Australian Speculative Poetry*, eds. P.S. Cottier & Tim Jones (Interactive Press).

Reed, Gabby. "The Devil Riding Your Back," *Liminality* 1.

Relf, Terrie Leigh. "Ode to Yon Gliesan Orbs, or No?" *Tales of the Talisman* 9:4.

Rich, Mark. "The Swooning," *Cascadia Subduction Zone* 4:2.

Rowan-Legg, Shelagh "Principles of Entropy," *Abyss & Apex*, January.

Schwader, Ann K. "Dark Energized," *Star*Line* 37.1.

Seybold, Grace. "Leap," *Star*Line* 37.1.

Simon, Marge. "Shutdown," *Qualia Nous*, ed. Michael Bailey (Written Backwards).

Simon, Marge, & Mary Turzillo. "Eolian Conscientia," *Sweet Poison* (Dark Renaissance Press).

Sloboda, Noel. "The Rat Queen," *Pembroke Magazine* 46.

Spriggs, Robin. "Revelation," *The Untold Tales of Ozman Droom* (Anomalous Books).

Sturner, Jason. "Intimate Universes," *Tales of the Talisman* 10:1.

Taaffe, Sonya. "A Bulgakov Headache," *Stone Telling* 10.

Takács, Bogi. "You Are Here / Was: Blue Line to Memorial Park," *Strange Horizons*, 11/24/14.

Turzillo, Mary. "Sonnet 65,000,000 BC," *Star*Line* 37.1.

Venable, Peter. "Dark Matter, Dark Mind," *Parody* 3:1.

Watkins, William John. "The Old Time Traveler's Song," *Asimov's Science Fiction*, January.

Woodward, Greer. "Cthulhu partners," *Halloween Haiku II*, ed. Lester Smith (Popcorn Press).

Wright, Sarah. "Let the Fire Decide," *Tales of the Talisman* 9:3.

Wytovich, Stephanie. "Dare I Keep the Body," *Mourning Jewelry* (Raw Dog Screaming).

Wytovich, Stephanie. "Eventually, You Become Immune," *Jamais Vu* 1.

Zable, Jeffrey. "Remembering Jean-Paul Sartre," *Chrome Baby*, Bairn 27.

Zinos-Amaro, Alvaro. "Conservation of Energy," *Apex Magazine*, August.

SPONSORS OF THE 2015 RHYSLING ANTHOLOGY

BENEFACTORS
Mary Soon Lee

SPONSORS
Elizabeth Bennefeld

SUPPORTERS
P. Andrew Miller
Greer Woodward

DONORS
David C. Kopaska-Merkel
Ann K Schwader

EDITOR'S NOTE

Some of the monsters, landscapes, and metaphors found within science fiction, horror and fantasy never fail to tickle the imagination. Whether in fiction or in poetry, the reader is often treated to surreal and alien vistas, reflections of inhumanity, ancient lands, and the new myths and legends from a literary culture continuing to grow and expand. That's just part of the joy of reading. The other part involves arguing, quite passionately, over which works go above and beyond to demonstrate the vitality of horror, science fiction, and fantasy literature. Think about it; we as readers argue about books nearly every day. We do it while having coffee with our friends, we send e-mails, we join discussions online, we post links to our favorite recently read poems on social media, and more—all in the name of sharing what we have discovered to be meaningful. Sometimes these discussions can get ugly. Sure, we can just as passionately talk about the work that thoroughly disappoints us. Either way, debating literature is something we all love to do.

That's what makes the SFPA *Rhysling Anthology* so unique and special every year. This book is unlike many other yearly fantasy, horror, or science fiction best-of collections. Outcomes have already been determined in those tomes. You start reading those outcomes—those selections—once you open the cover. The *Rhysling Anthology* is not the end of a story. Actually, it's just the middle part. Members have already nominated their favorite poems from the last year. The end of the tale comes later, after this volume sees print. Ultimately, SFPA members must individually whittle this book down to just two poems. As voting members, that is the fun part. How do you decide? How do you make those hard choices? Which poems do you dismiss outright? Which do you champion? Which do you read, reread, and puzzle over? As a non-voting reader, the joy is trying to prognosticate and guess which two pieces will ultimately cross the finish line for awards. A book like this always facilitates discussion over what is not only a good or a bad poem, but what makes a poem good or bad. Trust me, that is a good thing. So, in that regard, let the debate begin.

Rich Ristow
2015 Rhysling Chair

Rich Ristow was born in Bitburg, West Germany. He has also lived in the United Kingdom, Bermuda, Belgium, the Netherlands, West Virginia, North Carolina, and New Jersey. Currently, he teaches English at the Changzhou College of Information Technology in Jiangsu Province, China. He holds a MFA in poetry from the University of North Carolina at Wilmington and is a prior Rhysling winner. His books include *Estranged: Tales of Horror in Bermuda, Anthems for a Doomed Youth, Wood Life: A Poem, The Miswanted*, and others. He can be found online at richristow.com.

ABOUT THE RHYSLING AWARDS

In 1978, Suzette Haden Elgin founded the Science Fiction Poetry Association (SFPA), along with its two initial publications: the association's newsletter, *Star*Line*, and the *Rhysling Anthology*, the voting instrument of the Rhysling Awards.

*Star*Line* began as a forum and networking tool for poets with a shared interest in speculative poetry, from science-fiction verse to high-fantasy poems, from the macabre to straight science and associated mainstream genres such as surrealism, and is now a showcase for speculative poems and a venue for essays on speculative poetry and reviews of speculative poetry books.

The Rhysling Awards are named for the blind poet Rhysling in Robert A. Heinlein's short story "The Green Hills of Earth." Rhysling's skills were said to rival Rudyard Kipling's. In real life, Apollo 15 astronauts named a crater near their landing site "Rhysling," which has since become its official name.

The *Rhysling Anthology* serves as not only a voting instrument for the Rhysling Awards, but also as a representative collection of some of the best speculative poetry of the preceding year. The nominees for each year's Rhysling Awards are selected by the membership of the Science Fiction Poetry Association. Each member is allowed to nominate one work in each of the two categories: Best Short Poem (1–49 lines) and Best Long Poem (50+ lines). All nominated works must have been first published during the preceding calendar year. The Rhysling Awards are determined by vote of the SFPA membership from the nominated works reprinted in this voting tool, the *Rhysling Anthology*. The anthology allows the membership to easily review and consider all nominated works without the necessity of obtaining all the diverse publications in which the nominated works first appeared. The *Rhysling Anthology* is also available to purchase in print and .pdf format by anyone with an interest in this unique compilation of verse from some of the finest poets working in the field of speculative/science-fiction/fantasy/horror poetry; see sfpoetry.com/rhysling.html for more information.

The winning works are regularly reprinted in the *Nebula Awards Showcase* published by the Science Fiction and Fantasy Writers of America and are considered in the speculative field to be the equivalent in poetry of the awards for prose work—achievement awards given to poets by the peers of their own literature.

Printing and distribution of *The Rhysling Anthology* are paid for by the SFPA. If you would like to contribute to the organization so that we may continue to produce this and other publications and fund the organization's efforts, please send a check, made out to the Science Fiction Poetry Association, to:

SFPA Treasurer
PO Box 907
Winchester CA 92596

or donate online via PayPal to **SFPATreasurer@gmail.com**.

Adapted from *Star*Line* 12.5–6 (1989).

CONTENTS

SHORT POEMS FIRST PUBLISHED IN 2014 (59 poems)

LONG POEMS (40 poems)

Worlds Apart

Mary Alexandra Agner

I don't think the Moon wants
to go home. You have cosseted it,
given it cake and cookies,
admired its fullness as a function
of time. It has kept you up
late with its returned volley
of flattery and I desperately want
for you to come to bed,
warm depression in the mattress
beside me as we co-pilot into sleep.
From the darkness I hear your laughter
and know it has fooled you
through one more story, tenderly
wiping the dust from your eyes.
I'm a poor lover, voyeur
in my own home, unable to take
the stairs and step into the brilliance.
I believe in choice.
When you ran away with me
my metal heart nearly burst.
Choose again, choose me again.
Moon and spoon may rhyme
but we are worlds apart.

Main Sequence

Saira Ali

    For Michelle

None of the models fit.
Hammer our eccentricities away,
Discard the evidence trails we blaze,
Astronomers, try to force us into their tidy hypotheses
But we defied them all

I was thought to be a moon
Cold dark in indirected orbit around

You, burning brilliant gamma ray and neutrino core
Dazzled me

A moon can't survive its star's extinction
Drawn down into its gravity well
Knowledge, then, your best last gift
Which nevertheless I would return if ... (red shift)

I did not fold follow fall past the
Discontinuity
Heat rising stretching skin tight light seen through closed lids
Is my own therefore I must be a star.

Time and space warp shift twist under around through me
Nullity tangible altering my course yes, but,
Still I burn, traverse the vacuum
Forging and scattering new constellations
Spinning boiling turbulences dancing down my skin
Until that day my fuel is spent and I follow you down
Across that event horizon

The Delusions of Trees

David Barber

In the Book of Everything, between
the Psychology of Wood and Saprophobia,
is a chapter on the delusions of trees;

how they summered in fair Eden once,
one with the earth, the sun and the rain
before the coming of the quick,

whose hungers test a faith
of letting go and the green return.
Banished from their parent's shade,

trees know nothing of fathers
nor any arbour above. Convinced
the wind lifts prayers like pollen

to the bright horizons, their deity is the forest,
which is honoured even by the quick,
who nail its wood to their own dead god.

Pauli Neutrino Telescope, Antarctica, July 14ᵗʰ, 2033

David Barber

Particle-noir winds from Sagittarius
blow through the superconductor array
frozen deep beneath the Ross Ice Shelf,
howling like ghosts in the machine. Outside
it is 30 below. We huddle down
and eavesdrop on physics inventing itself.

Nearly two hundred thousand years ago,
veiled by the Clouds of Magellan, minds
lit candles in the dark; we rise to find
every screen dancing with neutrino spikes;
even the medium is a message
of vast technologies beyond mankind.

For thirty amphetamine hours we chase
the signal star, until a last tsunami
of neutrinos throb out of its stellar heart
as it goes nova. They saw it coming
and wanted to tell somebody something.
We have no idea where to start.

Africa wakened us to life and death,
and the guilty survivors were seized
by the mystery of it; they would sense
the land was alive and everywhere dense
with meaning; in time it would seem like home.
But suns burst with fathomless indifference

and nothing out there loves flesh that thinks.
The brightness fades, and with it an answer.
Our headphones hiss with the radio noise
of galaxies lost in time; we listen
late into the night for fleeting voices,
for someone to tell us it is otherwise.

Lost

F.J. Bergmann

The vidloop runs continuously: an extinct floater hovering before what looks almost like a blossom, also gone (recorder held by an unknown first colonist); the strange sun's spectrum, almost like Earth's, refracting through a glass-balloon shell, a riffle of prismatic wings. Gauge, measure, timestamp. What looks like hunger might be random movement, might be sex, might be the transfer of irrecoverable data. These lifeforms did not survive the cataclysm of our advent and are long-dead. Through an unopenable window into the past, something like a butterfly and something like a flower exchange something that is almost certainly not a kiss.

Science Fiction
[with apologies to Marianne Moore's "Poetry"]

Ruth Berman

I, too, dislike it: the claimed vast expanses of space viewed
   from the claustrophic confines of a spaceship
  where they feed on pills or powdered concentrates
  or at best grow food in hydroponic vegetable gardens
    where they have no room for trees
  and even each stretch of grass (being inedible)
    that gets allowed
  must pay its way in renewing the ship's oxygen.

Oh, the stars, the stars! salting the dark universe
    with lights in many colors
  and the planets we (assuming the invention of FTL,
  as sf mostly does assume it,
  or at least near-light near enough
    for relativity effects to kick in)
    will discover and explore
  (or our distant descendants,
  but that's an unpopular choice,
  so cryogenic sleep tends to get assumed
    if FTL isn't).

In the meantime, you must not expect to hug family or friends
  not there on board to crew the ship
    anytime soon,

and if FTL doesn't get assumed you mustn't
  expect to ever.
But if you assume it or if you explain how you assume
  it isn't
  you are
    necessarily
       interested in science fiction.

Maybe Waldo Had Syphilis

Matt Betts

I never found him. I looked. I did. Hours spent with a magnifying glass in one hand, a Sunny D in the other. Scouring faces, following his trail. It just wasn't my thing. Eventually, I gave up. Now that I'm older, I feel bad about it. I mean, what if Waldo was gravely ill and he didn't even know it. The whole purpose of the game might have been to locate him so a crack medical team could get him life-saving medication. Presumably, he's dead now. If my success was any indication.

But, you know, thinking about it, maybe that emergency medicine thing was a ruse. It sounds like an excuse mobsters would use in order to get me to lead them right to Waldo so they could deliver him a gruesome fate. Did he owe them money because of a terrible gambling problem? Was it a love triangle? I could see a guy like Waldo sleeping with a gangster's girlfriend. Unknowingly, of course.

I'm glad I didn't find him. Maybe he escaped with the young lady and they're living an honest life in Chicago or Orlando or Vegas. If I know Waldo, it's someplace crowded. He probably works in a mall or a fish market, an airport, maybe. Sounds like a decent life.

Unless … Maybe the criminals already got to him. Maybe that's why I couldn't find him in the first place. Dear God.

Suppose, finally, that Waldo was just an ass with no regard for anyone else's feelings. Suppose that he ran and ran for fun. Keeping one step ahead of his pursuers—friends, concerned citizens and well-wishers alike. Mimosas on the beach. A pint in the shadow of Big Ben.

I'm going to try again. Work harder to find Waldo. This time, I'll work day and/or night until I get it right. And when I see him, hidden in plain sight on the beach in Rio de Janeiro, standing between a stall selling umbrellas and an overturned candy cane delivery truck, I'll pull off his silly hat and those black glasses and I'll embrace him firmly.

"It's alright," I'll say. "You can come home. Your girlfriend is pregnant. You're going to be a father." And while he stands, speechless, doing math as to when he last saw his lost love, I'll slip on his disguise and fade into the pages, disappearing in a crowd at an Ohio State football game or the Mall of America. I'll let anonymity wash over me and begin a game of my own. Peanut butter and jelly on the Riviera, a Coke at the Kremlin.

The Cuckoo's Bride

Robert Borski

Because he knows she will abandon
their children to the care of others,
he eschews what nature tells him to look
for (plump feathers to warm his brood,
a beak and stamina for trawling worms,
a plethora of nursery tales converted to lilt),
and instead decides to cast his lot
with a scrawny little thing best known
for having mastered the mating songs
of dozens of other species; and so as he
mounts her, he makes love, pseudo-
polygamously, to wren, sparrow, thrush,
and (scarily) crow—all the brides
come home to roost, so to speak,
each and every one a potential mother
to his scattered egglings, past, present,
and yet to see light through the cracked
dome of their outsourced shells.

Septuagenarian Flashback

Bruce Boston

Stumbling into the humid
jasmine-scented dark
from a midnight cinema
playing an iconic art film
rife with sidewalk cafes

and laconic actors whose
monochromatic silences
confabulate to a toxic
conundrum of pale angst
and lost existential loves,

my venerable thoughts
segue to foggy mornings
in a metropolis by the bay,
wandering the slantwise
streets of stoned youth

and the fleeing tendrils
of a Guatemalan high,
a great golden bridge
aglow with the blurred
headlamps of early traffic

rising out of the mist,
glittering like some fabled
and fantastic behemoth
that could carry me to
a chameleon tomorrow.

there are signs of Faerie everywhere

G. Sutton Breiding

there are signs of Faerie everywhere
in traces of lunar-pink and candy-gold
glittering in giddy clouds above the dancing streams
where the emerald lips of fashion nymphs
leave their luminous kisses on the air
impossibilities haunt me
like the antiquitous Tomorrows
I never knew
in the 1950s hills of West Virginia
so I learned to make paper from my dreams
and ink from my astonishments
the roadside asters still take me all the way
to Algol
and the scent of Martian verses
still rings in this kitchen at the edge of Time
where I drink my human coffee
from night's bright cup
of final, phantastic fictions

Stalking a Wizard

Michael Canfield

Gawky,
yes.
Ungainly ... never.
Unkempt? A little perhaps,

as a weathered oaken desk is unkempt,
its cubbies bursting with scribbled sheaves:
a lean old magik with the city's dust on his heels,
and the ink of conjures beyond number beneath his
nails.

White hair, sharp as lightning,
face, a storm-battered coastline,
shoulders higher than alps,
spine, a gnarled, unbowed, cherrywood staff:
at the city of Saint Francis
in the street of the Turk,
he passes close as night.

You follow.
Certainly you follow
the Master of Unknown,
Weird Teller of Tales, to his home,
watch him fade into the black edifice.

That can't be it, you think,
not so small a building, not so narrow a street,
not after so many adventures.
High seas,
dark hearts,
wandering millennia,
have brought him here, near the last:
a solitary room in the Tenderloin.

You check the names on the mailboxes,
run your finger over the raised letters
to be sure: *F. Leiber*, it read, it did.
But the spell is cast, never to be undone.

Even in a northern forest, thirty-odd years later,
after a little oatmeal and a boiled egg,
his spell lingers
and you write this poem.

Dragon to Centauri

Beth Cato

building a dragon
involves more than sinew or scales
it begins with the heart
cold fusion, pumping ventricles

a skeleton of gray steel
coiling corridors of the veins
a skin cool and smooth
eyes that stare into oblivion
across this blackened vacuum
and fire from its lips, always fire
a quiet and soundless flame
to immolate foes and keep safe
the charges nestled within its belly
when ready to take wing
this dragon will roar
as its wings scrape the stars

A Work In Progress

G.O. Clark

When they blast off,
the great starships are like
heroic symphonies—

Beethoven or Tchaikovsky.

Free of Earth's gravity,
solar sails unfurled, their song
turns to minimalism—

the gradual musical changes of
a Riley, Reich, or Glass.

Passing through our
solar system, each planet triggers
a symphonic movement—

that classical pomp of Holst.

At destination's end,
across our star-studded galaxy,
a new world silence,

a blank score waiting for some
latter-day Dvorak.

Short Forms

David Clink

I dream I am on a parallel Earth where they do not use any short forms. There are no initials, no contractions, no abbreviations. My computer stops working, so I buy a new International Business Machine. I log on, someone sends me a joke, and I find myself rolling on the floor laughing my ass off. Later I go to a party where everyone wears polyvinyl chloride. It was one of *those* kinds of parties. One woman tells me she uses self-contained underwater breathing apparatus when diving the Barrier Reef. Her favourite poets are Edward Estlin Cummings and Thomas Stearns Eliot. I tell her my favourite authors are Herbert George Wells and John Ronald Reuel Tolkien. I find that I miss the ability to be brief, that contractions give us more time to get to know each other. I want to return to my world where there are lasers and radar, a world where there is the promise of an FTL drive, a world where you can write a letter that ends with *PS: I love you.*

After hours in the op shop

P.S. Cottier

After 'The Pawnbroker's Shop' by Charles Dickens

At last the door is closed, and down we all slither down
from our thin metal supports. Smelling of mothballs,
of sweat, of lavender, we hump towards the centre
of the shop, now cleared of customer and clerk.
Oh, we are become Medusa, but Medusa with tongues
instead of snakes, with a pillow-clump of ourselves
for head. I can taste a soupçon of peppermint
as I caress the mauve blouse that twines itself
around me. I sense the woman who wore it once
undoing sweets in church, feel her boredom assuaged
by that little marsupial jump of taste buds. Her attention
blooms back to the parson's numbing drone.

     Mauve tastes me;
the weekend scales that decorated my plaid sleeves,
impart a certain memory of trout. I feel her feel
the rough arms of Jack, scratch my khaki arms
as he used his to clean his catch. She hums, and is it
that never-ending ballad about 'The Wild Colonial Boy'
mild Jack whistled crookedly through a weekend smile.
She has caught it, firm as a plump rainbow fish,

netted by my weft and weave; now passed on.
It mixes with her *former*'s hymns; angels and fish entwined.
Like octopi we squirm, and taste the picnics of memories
spread like a smorgasbord amongst us. The sad violet
of a young child lost, the acrid orange anger of thug,
the occasional honey of the plainly good.

                   That last one wore jeans
so ugly and ordinary they might strut down a catwalk,
if fashion were to do mere patched practicality.
Denim and I meet, and recognise a tint of mutual past
as we taste each other's recipe. Perhaps we are snakes,
after all, shedding onto each other a skin of *before*;
a confetti of *used to* or a dandruff of *was*.
Hats are certainly not unknown, here, amongst us.
They scoop character, thickly, direct from the scalp.

After a night of experiment, we climb back onto our hangers.
The op shop opens at ten. Some will go out on new backs,
acquiring new chapters;
                  editing themselves to the library of skin.

[An op shop, short for opportunity shop, is the Australian name for a thrift shop.]

Keziah [Nahab] Mason

Cardinal Cox

Brought to stand trial in infamous Salem town
After torture she told a tale of black pacts
Strange midnight rituals and some terrible acts
No-one caught her small familiar Jenkin Brown

The great books of conjuring with circles inscribed
Convinced judge that for her crimes she would have to pay
Yet they found her dirty low cell empty one day
No-one suggested the county's gaoler was bribed

Some say that she still walks beneath alien stars
Found other directions tangled in atom hearts
Understood how to move herself from place to place

Her skin though still carries noble justices scars
While her mathematics describe unseen part
Saw four-dimensional brane within higher space

Neuroanatomy Practical

Tim Craven

Smaller than you thought.
More like your idea of a dog's.
You cup it softly. Your thumb fidgets
over the fissure of a temporal lobe.
You lift it up to the side of your head
and imagine your own, sitting in there—
firing, immortal.
If you were to lob it against the wall,
would it crumble or shatter
or liquefy or combust or bounce
back into your hands, intact?
When she (sixty-six, Caucasian, lymphoma)
donated it to science, was this the promised
afterlife? You consider biting into it
as you would a peach—and, were it not
for the toxic preservative, you might.
In ten years' time you will think
what a privilege it was to hold that brain,
brim-filled with tomato soup recipes and original sin
and smells of late summer and oboe lessons
and self-taught Italian and the night sky:
The Plough, The Bear, The Big Dipper.

I Imagine My Mother's Death

Bryan D. Dietrich

I imagine my mother's death. It is curiouser
than I thought. It wears a waistcoat and gloves,
a great gold watch on a proper chain. It wears
a beaver hat. It is worried about being late.
My mother's death does not smell like carrots
or little girls or rabbit holes. It wanders white
chapels, back alleys, the market's blackest shadows,
black as baby carriages. It knows how to cut meat,
how to lure its prey with the promise of money,
sex, strawberries. It smells of strawberries and, if
only faintly, formaldehyde. My mother's death
puts on its gloves and goes out for the night.
It finds a woman walking alone in the dark.

It hails her like a cab, enters her like a cab, offers
to help her paint the town red. She agrees, wanting
a way out, a waistcoat perhaps, a gold chain.
She dreams of carrots and rabbit holes, craves
even the maddest of hatters, someone to call her
Queen. When it is done with her, it wipes its knife
on the bib it has brought, then goes in search
of another. Another. They are all my mother.

Stephen Hawking

Bryan D. Dietrich

You awaken to find your wife gone from bed.
She's always been hot. So hot, once, she made
the image of a body on your inflatable camping
mattress. But now that she's vanished, her heat
is missing, her imprint fading fast. You wonder
where she's gone, what she's left, and discover
the urge to go outside, to stand, unnatural, under
the stars. You bring, to your surprise, two beers.
In the yard, Stephen Hawking waits. You find
him there between wrought-iron and crabapple.
You hand him his beer and, not ungenerously,
he neglects to mention your nakedness. His own
clothes hang from his frame like his face hangs
from his bones, his eyes more volatile than you
ever imagined. His voice comes slowly, like
a broken fax. Stephen Hawking tells you there is
a hole in space. It is a billion light-years across.
It is cold. The hole he describes lies ten billion
light-years away. It holds no matter, no dark matter,
but, he says, it is filled with what makes us expand.

Beware of the Dog

James S. Dorr

Sure, we've all heard it before,
how every full moon he gets out of control,
but any Saturday night in this burg
gets a little bit heavy.
Besides most of the bars

don't even let pets in,
no matter whether they're dogs or wolves—
not even seeing-eye pooches for blind folks—
and by Monday morning we're all so hung
that who even remembers?
So the thing is, sure, exercise some caution
when something growls at you,
maybe even stay in your car
until it lopes past,
but come the next work week
it's "How's it going, Charlie,"
when you pass his station at the plant
down the row from your own,
never mind what's the moon phase.

A Universe

Timons Esaias

Properly, it should be
seductive
—repay all the
trouble
of perception.

It should have no
beginning, must
at the very start
be already in
motion;
and no end.

Its theme should be accessible.

Whether it should have Time
is a question;
the pathos
and Death, its companion,
so often betray
poor taste.

Properly, it should
resonate
—clear; like all the
bells ever cast,
intertwined,
purified.

The Peal Divers

Francesca Forrest

They dive to the drowned city
Dive at Lauds and Vespers
Down to the lost cathedral
St. Florian of Inundations
St. Michael of the Depths
They come for the glossolalia
Of the tongueless bells

The peal divers trap
That mute polyphony
In the cage of their ribs
In the nacre of their hearts
And then ascend
To shouts and acclamations
And kneel, to let the golden ax
Split wide their chests
That the silent, holy song
May flood the land.

Extinction

Joshua Gage

After George Bilgere

I sit on the surrendered beach at twilight,
the best hour to catch them,
just before the sun glissades behind the horizon.
And there, beyond a distant wave,

is a Humpback Whale. *Megaptera novaeangliae.*
A triumph of water, breaching like the moon.

But I am lying.

There is no whale. There cannot be
a whale. There have been no whales
in these waters for decades.
This is a whale-free world,
a planet all whaled out, thoroughly
de-whaled.

I just want an excuse to whisper
whale,
which, as we all know, happens to be
among the top dozen softest words
in the English language. *Whale*.

So, as an ecological service, I rise
to the whaleless tide, within earshot
of the Massachusetts Turnpike
and its cathedrals of tunnels,
quietly praying the word *whale*.

Elephants in the Alley

Terry A. Garey

In the dream my mother and I
hold each other—
sobbing with exhaustion—
the menopause fairy
has cursed us with insomnia.
I'm so tired
she cries into the cotton nighty
on my shoulder.
I know, I know, I croon into her hair.
An old friend comes into the room,
points to the window.
Look, he cries, just look!
In the alley I see circus elephants
passing through on the way
from the train to the Big Top.
Mom, look!
Elephants in the alley—
You can see them between the garages!
Startled, she sees them,
looks at me,
sees me, and at last she understands
what we've been missing.
We laugh like sisters and watch the elephants,
we play cards all night,
sing, tell jokes, get cracker crumbs in the bed.
Finally we sleep together on top of the covers,
dream of being kids.
In the alley, elephants keep walking to the Big Top.

It's a Universal Picture

Gwynne Garfinkle

1

I grew up loving witches:
peaked black hats and broomsticks for flight,
Bewitched and books about the Salem witch trials.
One Halloween I asked my dad to make me up.
He worked on me with pencil and putty,
then I looked in the mirror and burst into tears.
I'd wanted to be Elizabeth Montgomery.
He'd made me a warty hag.

2

Somehow my dad knew I would love
those black-and-white monster movies.
They didn't scare me:
Karloff and Lugosi, Colin Clive and Dwight Frye
(Clive died young of TB,
Frye of a heart attack, riding a bus),
Lon Chaney Jr. sorrowfully turning werewolf,
Gloria Holden as Dracula's Daughter
trying to fight her nature.
I watched them on TV Saturdays
before sessions in the dentist's chair,
my teeth pulled from overcrowded, crooked rows,
the taste of blood in my mouth.

3

When I was grown,
my bedridden dad, ravaged
and rewritten,
transformed by Parkinson's,
would snarl like Karloff's monster,
and I, in horror, turn away.

Field Notes

Lola Haskins

1

Myrmecia sanguinea (Wheeler, 1916)

Thousands, perhaps hundreds of thousands lit on the black-thorn bushes atop Mount Armour. Then, struggling balls of males formed around each mating pair until one by one the balls collapsed. And, as their scurrying contents rose up the sides of my boots, even I, a man of science, was afraid.

*

Myrmicia rubra (Farron-White, 1876)

He saw clouds of ants gyrating in the air above a small beech tree near Stonehenge, their paths and intersects like the red dodder that lays its tiny blossoms over gorse. Then the ants spiraled upwards like a tree gone to flame and when his cheeks turned hot enough, he joined the others, dancing around the stones.

2

Ants who enslave other ants eventually become incapable of doing anything but fighting and preening and would, if not for the work of their prisoners, starve. E.O. Wilson says there is no conclusion to be drawn from this.

*

Certain beetles introduce themselves to passing ants by raising their abdomens to be licked—rather like a dog offering his bottom to another dog—and releasing a tranquilizing ooze. Then, since the pheromes they emit remind the potential host of his own, they are ceremoniously transported into that worthy's chambers and for the rest of their lives, fed whenever they tap a passing worker with an antenna and present their mouths. Some of these freeloading beetles even change their quarters in winter. Bert Hölldobler, writing in *Scientific American*, remains carefully in the realm of insects.

Before You Were a Vampire

irving

Before you were a vampire, we sat
on the porch swing Sunday afternoons,
listening to the radio, through the window.

Before you were a vampire, I thought
I would like to take up cave-diving, or
rock-climbing or anything, just to say I did.

Before you were a vampire, the kids
still found time to visit most holidays.
We spoiled their children greedily.

Before you were a vampire, we talked
about the great vacations we would take
when we retired. Greece. Bali. Cool places.

Before you were a vampire, I was saving
for a refrigerator. We really wanted a new car
but it wouldn't keep the food cold.

Before you were a vampire, you knew
the names of all the stars in the sky,
and all the people who lived on our street.

Before you were a vampire, I didn't know
you could reload used shotgun shells with
minced garlic and blessed shrapnel.

Before you were a vampire, we had a dog.

After the Changeling Incantation

John Philip Johnson

To become a goose
had seemed important, earlier,
when he made the change.
A gray goose for some reason, fat,
with the ability to lift above
the archers' arrows,
fly past the leafless autumn trees,
and cross the bowl of the mountain valley,
beyond those far peaks.

There was a mission—
to get something,
or to return with someone—
some reason to be a goose
other than just gooseness,
other than filling your wings with sky—

Hands drop the wand;
feathers cannot pick it up.
We forget when we change
we become something else.
Things mean differently.
He circled the great alpine woods,
forgetting. There, below,
knotted in the trees,
were the plottings of men,
creatures like little gods,
with their endless violence upon things.
They make such noise. They wail and bleed.
It is no place for a goose.
It is no place for one who can find
north and south within his body
and know which one to choose.

After "Dark Matter"

Herb Kauderer

For Timons Esaias

monsters are euphemisms
for the mindless hatred
of right-thinking zombies

and zombie movies are a celebration
of their fictional destruction

so that society can look away from the
brain-craving horde that shambles among us

and feel subliminal satisfaction as if
the zombies were really being dealt with

After "Signs You're in Trouble"

Herb Kauderer

For Mary Turzillo

1) One day the comics page is no longer funny.
2) The next day the comics page is printed in a language you don't read.
3) Your balcony levitates next to the living room but is no longer actually attached to the building.
4) Your husband wears sunglasses to bed.
5) You start wearing sunglasses to bed, too, but yours are rose-colored. It doesn't help.
6) The DVR has somehow become filled with home movies of your childhood.
7) You do not appear in any of the home movies.
8) Your child plays on an imaginary computer & prefers it to you.
9) Your cat is a space alien.
10) Your child laughs at your cat's jokes most of which are about removing your brain.
11) Your husband invites you to the LaBrea Tar Pits for dinner. No food is involved.
12) Jupiter is demoted from planetary status to "old windbag."
13) All the street signs in your neighborhood are replaced with the Latin names of dragons.
14) You don't read Latin.
15) Your neighbors are replaced by dragons.
16) Your condo is surrounded by neighbors drinking gasoline.
17) A beat-up UPS truck driven by Joe the Old Poet delivers boxes of poetry.
18) S'mores toasted over burning poetry bring neighbors together in a bonding experience.
19) While the neighbors are bonding you try to sneak out to the floating balcony where you find your husband & cat are waiting with trepanning drills & bone saws.
20) The night is still young ...

Heere ther be Gods

David C. Kopaska-Merkel

after swallowing the moons
Ghŭlach slurped rings and asteroids
shook comets out of the ecliptic
with its mighty mane
licked the largest gassy orb
to a rocky lump
and flared its massy wings

telescopes showed it moving
out into deep space
maw agape baleen-whale style
a sigh of relief was heard just before
a mephitic discharge shot through
the inner system
cosmic residue, refractory, toxic, and opaque
blotted out the sun

Attic Dust

Sandi Leibowitz

weightless as words
　　—and who knows the heft
　　　　of words better than I?—
　I drowse, unformed,
　　　　my crumbs unvisited

Long ago,
my creator kneaded Vltava clay
　to a lump less lovely
　　　than Sunday's challah

Scattering letters and crooning
　the secret name of God,
　　　Papa Loew spelled me alive.

Holy somnambulist,
　I walked unthinking
　　　acting only as he willed.

Till one day myself
　awoke my self,

daring disobedience.

With a swipe of wool sleeve,
   Papa Loew erased my word,
      my breath,
         reduced me again
           to lump of clay.

   Below the synagogue's rafters,
the backwards-racing clock,
     I sleep
        while Pařížská Street laughs or screams
          to the beat of axes or hammers
            Tourists shuffle murmuring
               past prayer-books and gravestones

But what is truth? What is death?
  Emet, met
What is life? What is sleep?

In dreams my tongue
     untwists
and I hold forth
erudite as a rabbi,
charming as a matinée idol.

No longer lumbering,
    my grace outslinks
the mayor's cat.

My mud, Brother Adam, like yours
decays to dust.

And
this dust
     dreams.

Dualities

Rose Lemberg

The universal flow of prime numbers
unleashed from your/my sleeves
surrounds you/me in pillars of light. I/you never
understood math, you/I never
knew much about architecture, languages,

the processing of speech into data and storysong, that
wordshaping that anchored me/you in the ground. You/I navigate
between stars with motion/no motion
that exists outside timeflow and yet bound in it; the manifold, unfolding
along the pathways of the veins.

You/I understand little
of the laws that frame me/you, and yet
we broke up with the fathers of our children, wept/silently grit teeth
over our sons' disabilities, kept quiet/spoke
over the screams of the body, took
new lovers
in an attempt/absolution over despair/despair.

you/I, emergent and merged
through this language, this silence, this memory of forgetting,
through kinetic numbers and the accumulation of sung lives:
I/you, traversing this desert/this space
shall speak/sing with hope ascendant.

Falling upward, you/I will not merge
into a cohesion not of our designing. We will exist/be
wound against each other in pillars of light,
like DNA or prime numbers,
like rivers,
like storysongs into the earth,
at the exit/entrance to the worlds that are becoming.

Landwork

Rose Lemberg

You say this stitchery is women's work, not for warriors,
even if they are women. You say,
whoever heard of land-stitchery? But if it is important,
then it's warrior work. With no strength in your limbs
to swing a sword, how can you do whatever it is you do? It has to be
unimportant, busywork
with too much ornament,
a waste of everyone's time.

Listen, each dawn and sunset,
each day and darkness I don't see you. I only notice
your words because my friends repeat them.
Listen, what you say has no significance.

They slash, I piece together
that which has been slashed and that which has not been.
The seen and unseen meld in my hands,
I make lands from scraps,
I make these lands flow into each other,
embrace like sisters within the strictures of my thread.

When my arms are too painful for daywork, I ask
if it pleases the clouds to make rainshirts,
if it pleases the meadows to sprout flowercoats and bedding,
if it pleases the rocks to piece me a belt.
Rarely do I ask. I am patient
in my coat of fallen leaves from yesteryear,
in my shoes of nothing much.

That pattern in which every leaf is adorned,
the fine stitchery of sap,
the entwinement of rivers
all that you've called redundant
is the blood which flows, well-ornamented,
through your veins in threads I chose.
The land, too,
doesn't notice your opinions
as it washes your meat into mud,
makes a cat's cradle from your bones.

But I will always be here
under the sky's benevolent wail,
sifting stones with the patience of water,
as significant as the space between breaths.

Cinderella Breast

Sandra J. Lindow

At the Palace, my paper gown
opens down the front,
exposing me to scrutiny
in a rapidly retreating anesthetized world:
"Why yes, Cinderella, you can have a life,"
Grand Vizier Medical said,
"but first we conquer that cancer:"
two lumps in my left breast,
entwining secret metastasis.
"Bibbety, bobbety, boo, make it go," I said.

But this sterile Kingdom
Isn't Blue Fairy blessed:
No magic but the sticky-slick passing
of a surgeon's knife, mastectomy
and the beginnings of a promised
reconstruction, an alien
gazebo built under my skin,
normal saline added in,
cobble stone mockery of a breast
that presses heavily on my chest,
hampering my breathing
and making my heart race.
"Take it out," I said.

Folklorists write
that the Woman's Journey
may start with a maiming,
far easier said on the page
than felt in the heart's center:
Heroism is lonely and hurts.
My old breast burned
toward inflagration. The fire is out,
but now that the parting's over,
I sleep unevenly on a cold hearth.

Losing more than a shiny shoe,
the ashes of health darken
my demeanor, and I see
a briared forest path twisting
into impenetrable dark.
The North Wind blows,
an ineffable animal howl.
I clench the hearth stones
awaiting the Chemical Bear
to slash and shred my quaking house.

[untitled]

Lauren McBride

daydreaming

bad idea

during telepathic exchange

Common Language

Elizabeth R. McClellan

Venutians never had a double modal
before they came south.

Children who think Jackson, Mississippi is humid
say *We might could* in dialect that shudders
at stacking it was never meant to accommodate.

Tlang's brood-nurse came down to see the fall colors,
near about fell out when she heard Kendall
neutralizing lax vowels, the stresses all out of order—*but
remarkably good* [hive-language-fourth-quadrant-dialect]
for a grub–and a [blue-neighbor-planet] *grub no less…!*

Ann Marie emailed their mother three months
after the interplanetary move:

*Hot, like New Orleans in August,
but worse—except the clouds cut the glare
to nothing. Ten times the lightning,
never rain—and no porch-sitting,
not without a p-suit. I miss a good breeze.*

Sxrit finds daffodils make her faintly nauseated,
remind her of larva jelly gone rancid.
They told her about rain, but not
how fast clouds roll in, how the first cold drop
can startle you to screaming,
nor the smell, the taste of water when it falls.

Even more incomprehensible than
when to say *y'all* and when *all y'all*,
though her neighbors are gracious at
such small mistakes, say *oh honey,
never you mind all that now.*

Gdryh's senior thesis, critically received,
traces cross-migration patterns,
suggests a connection with
gender neutral second person plurals.

He presses a sprig of dogwood
for his lover's scrapbook back home—
Chris misses spring in Memphis,
however much he loves the endless days,

the whipping winds, the hazy skies
of this new home place.

In Vicksburg or on Venus, a common question,
drawled, clicked or signed:

Hello, friend,
Some [outside-conditions] *we're having.*

The Time of Last Scattering

Lynette Mejía

"The Time of Last Scattering" refers to the moment, roughly 380,000 years
after the Big Bang, when the universe cooled sufficiently to allow matter and
radiation to separate, freeing light particles to move unimpeded through a newly
transparent cosmos.

I was a photon once;
a child of the light,
a particle and a wave,
frenetic; incipient, all
wild nights and vainglory.
Freed from the restraint
of the time before, I took it
upon myself to measure
the fragmented universe,
my brothers and sisters in chaos.

Even as a child I was bold,
declaring the need for quantum recalibration,
paving highways relative to paths
I'd charted alone. From the vacuum I pulled
intimations of the impending, creating
maps and star charts; birthing tenuous, threaded
blueprints of solar flares and ray guns,
whistling tunes carried on webs of ether. It was hot, then,
hotter than now, and we were abrasive,
because that's what's called for when you bound
a universe.

Only in retrograde do I consider
the wisdom of endless expansion,
the flip side of freedom.
Where once we burned
bright signal fires and bold staccato waves
now there is only dust,

only the twinkle of the already dead.
Trembling with an anticipation
I thought I'd left behind, I wait
beside their bodies, a solitary mourner
haunting spaces between novae,
where Doppler shifts leave crimson stains
echoing soundlessly forever.

Marvel Word Problems

P. Andrew Miller

If Spider-Man can lift 15 tons, can jump over 20 feet, has reflexes 15 times faster than normal, but can't save the people he loves, how do you measure regret?

If Aurora leaves the convent flying at Mach 3 heading east and her brother Northstar leaves Montreal at Mach 5 heading south but stops in New York to come out, what is the speed of acceptance?

If Black Bolt's voice caused the death of his parents and cost his brother his sanity, and he wants to tell Medusa, his wife, he loves her, what is the price of a whisper?

If Apocalypse attacks New York at 5:33 and the X-Men save the day at 8:22 and the mutant protests start at 8:30, what time does the hate stop?

If the Scarlet Witch can control probabilities and marry a synthezoid and have children yet go insane and kill her friends in the Avengers, what are the chances of love in the Age of Ultron?

Odyssey

Kim L. Neidigh

For centuries Major Nathan Edwards
Drifted through the void of space,
Face frozen in startled death,
Eyes unseeing the glories of Creation
Unfolding in the emptiness around him.
He floated past a world of darkness
Where purple lemurs warred perpetually
With hordes of black arachnids,
He became enveloped
By a cloud of sentient gas
That spat him out in disgust,
Journeyed near an ancient derelict

Whose crew still screamed insanely
As their souls slowly leached into hyperspace.
The Crimson Comet once presented itself
To his sightless orbs
As its accompanying micrometeors
Ripped through his frigid flesh.
After untold millennia his wanderings ended
As his tattered and forgotten remains
Were caught in the gravity well of a red star.
A brief flash marked his final passing.
There were no mourners at his cremation.

Queen of Cups
A. J. Odasso

The cards say I'll be leaving, tell me I'll travel south,
likely settle. Four long months of a single message
mustn't prove false, or my compass is shot. How cruel
has time proved that I must run; what love have I become
while sitting so still? *Queen of Cups*, they whisper, *Page
of Vessels Yet Unfilled*. I'll hail my favorite constellation
with these dazzling, inventive suits I've played for keeps
if this chance would but have me. Question your heart,
little sister, and the cards will find you; do speak truly
if the Page should pass her cup down your quiet row.

Morning Sickness
Aimee Ogden

"Morning sickness",
people called it:
but each time they make port
the ship's clock resets
to match planetside hours.
Nine at night on Europa,
oh-seven-hundred on Mars, and
half past three when they put into Titan:
she finds herself turning green
at all hours of day and night.
Captain tells her she needs to
Stay. Put.

next time they hit dirt, and she agrees
(no intention of following through).
Her baby's baptism will be to arrive
halfway between worlds:
her implicit prayer that this child
will share her wanderlust;
that her son will be a companion in travel,
that he will not be an anchor.

At the Dark Matter Zoo

Simon Petrie

At the Dark Matter Zoo,
the beasts are caged in mystery,
tended with conjecture,
described with imprecision.

At the Dark Matter Zoo,
I'm advised photography seldom captures
the wonder (or, indeed, anything).

At the Dark Matter Zoo,
visitors thrill to catch perhaps-sight of
the stygiosaurs, shadow jackals, Schrödinger cats;
with only the souvenir stand palpable.

At the Dark Matter Zoo,
it's possible some enclosures are completely
empty,
their charges escaped
or simply never

At the Dark Matter Zoo,
even the exits
are marked none too clearly;
refreshments are unfulfilling;
the Site Map does not serve.

At the Dark Matter Zoo,
the ghosts of the dodo,
the thylacine, the Falklands wolf, the Haast eagle,
I sought in vain.

The devil riding your back

Gabby Reed

ten years old when the ocean spat beasts and they
walked the world with strides the size of cities and i hid
i coward-cowered from the noise of it and the dark
until they crouched into mountains and slept left us
shaken shabby in their footprints, peering out.

fire and rubble and everyone died. i
grew up. we built houses, went to school,
wore swimsuits, got haircuts, grew old.

when i was a young girl vital,
unstooped, no concrete dust in my hair,
on my skin, no glass underfoot,
no dry shale taste, i was face-up,
i was raw strong, i sang, i belted.
now i'm hours under the writing desk
staying very, very still, with muffling
curtains, with scythe smile ghosts i'm
holding onto clock face hands to weather
hydraulic hammers, the kick and the sway,
the ground's grand betrayal, the city
and the beast's heel pinching like a mouth,
our bodies, teeth ground together so i

became so small a mote a molecule. i lived
the innocuous life i soft-stepped i folded down
and down, careful, prepared, precise.

everyone knows that the mountains are dead and i know that
they're alive drool and blood and fire deep inside inhale ten years
exhale twenty i am ready the taste of grit under my tongue didn't
fade the gaze on the nape of my neck never left me alone ever
since they were dead i am grown and this time i'll be ready.

Dark Energized

Ann K. Schwader

The most is mystery, not on our side
But otherwise, a darkness tearing dark
& light alike apart. Nowhere to hide:

The most is mystery, not on our side
Like matter's shadow sister, but a tide
That undertows the stars. Past vision's mark,
The most is mystery—not on our side,
But otherwise. A darkness tearing dark.

Leap

Grace Seybold

Waking is slow. The frozen throat forgets
a pulse once beat inside it. There were dreams
of screaming. Limbs come free. The body seems
to have survived, and I, inside, and yet—

And yet the ship is motionless. We meant
to wake in orbit, seven centuries gone
from Earth, to land and settle. It's gone wrong;
we've stopped far out, dark, cold, our venture spent—

And yet the planet sparkles. Strings of light
mark cities. Signals tell of people near
who, decades past, outracing light, came here
to wait for us on our unneeded flight.

Here where we thought we'd be the first to roam
our children's children's children call us home.

Shutdown

Marge Simon

They barred the library doors today.
Men in uniform stand patrol, armed and ready
their lantern jaws firm, lips a straight line.
Stoic women, also armed, jog up and down
the block, buttocks moving like pistons.

Someone dashes from a building
a hand-held reader clutched close.
Shots are fired; I don't stay to find out more.

I've packed the car with books, little room for else.
It is my car, his gift to buy my silence,
to make up for the bruises real and otherwise;

never marry a politician who has no use
for literature, has no use for a wife that does.

Eagles have left their nests to vultures
the barren palm trees whimper for their loss
there are ceaseless storms, mud is everywhere
while two legged insects multiply unchecked

The car radio plays Ibsen, bassoons herald the trolls.
I roll down the window, taking a deep breath
outside of Pyr Gynt's Hall of the Mountain King,
foreboding notes of the oboe, a palpable stench of fear.
Am I leaving that, or taking it with me …

The Rat Queen

Noel Sloboda

We wanted something to die
that night we neighborhood boys
gathered behind the storage facility.

It was littered with black plastic
rattraps we broke open
to expose poison inside. We basted

our dark wish with peanut butter
and left the concoction between units
then fled into blackness.

Scotty spotted our victim first—
not a rat but a possum,
belly slung low, slapping the concrete.

We held our breath, reddening
as she waddled up to the bait
and choked it down.

The possum gurgled and convulsed.
For a moment, we feared
she might bolt. Instead she dropped

and babies spilled out of her.
The possum's mouth gaped
as if she had something to say.

But her progeny had already scattered.
As soon as the last had gone,
rats emerged from nowhere;

they gathered round the body,
standing on back legs, heads bowed.
They listened to a tall rat

deliver a eulogy praising the possum
who had sacrificed herself to reveal
threats intended for all.

When the speech ended, the rats
solemnly raised the possum
high above their heads

and bore her into the night,
delicately handling her as though
she might break again.

Revelation

Robin Spriggs

He tried for nearly half an hour to stabilize the wobbly table outside the coffee shop on that otherwise perfect day half a hundred autumns ago. First he ascertained the offending leg. Then he tried placing various things under its suspended foot: a folded-into-a-square napkin, a wadded-into-a-ball cup sleeve, a stacked-into-a-plinth ennead of castaway cigarette butts. But the problem would not be solved; it leapt from leg to leg, from foot to foot, defying reason (or what passed for it), thwarting physics (or his understanding of it), mocking prayer (or his skill at it). Maybe it's not the table, he thought. Maybe it's the patio. Or the lay of the land. Or the tilt of the earth. Or. Or. Or. He sat and considered the matter for half another hour. Then he took out a pen, wrote something down on a napkin, placed his cup of coffee—half full, half empty, all tepid—on top of it, and departed the lines of this narrative, never to be mentioned again. Later, as a dull-eyed barista in pigtails cleared the cluttered table, the napkin blew away—unread, unacknowledged—baring its words to the wind: "It's me," it said. "It's me. It's me it's me it's me ..."

Intimate Universes

Jason Sturner

Inspired by the theory that cosmic branes (of a multiverse) can touch and influence one another

Their "kiss" lasted but one millionth of a second,
though truly timeless and spared of angels; a mere gleam
in the dreaming eye of Pan; the first quiver of life in primordial ooze.
A singularity popped off the tongue of a howling black hole,
expanded where nascent gods toss rose petals over looping,
cosmic currents, shot plasma-fire blue into the nothing of our universe—
a universe silent as an ash-covered opera—until the chaos of cooling atoms
induced space-time and spark, lending symphonic gravity
to the tenacity of evolution, to the intangibles of consciousness.

A Bulgakov Headache

Sonya Taaffe

No wonder he had such headaches
with a dictator always trying to get into his head
while his devils tried to get out,
my nervous writer, sleepless in a nightmare,
stories like cigarette ash on his cuffs.
No wonder if his books racked him like fevers,
clanged in his dreams like the guns at Kiev.
No wonder my head burns, thinking on Misha
half blind by the end of it, still seeing too much.

You Are Here / Was: Blue Line to Memorial Park

Bogi Takács

This is a visual poem with animations. This linearized version features a verbal description of the animations, and the full text of the poem.
The original animated version can be found at http://www.strangehorizons.com/2014/20141124/takacs-p.shtml .

Description: First, only the "You Are Here" segment is displayed. Then, the words of the "You Are Here" segment disappear one by one and reappear underneath in a new configuration. They form the segment "Was: Blue Line to Memorial Park". The two segments feature the exact same words, only in different arrangements.

You Are Here

You need to take the Blue Line to Memorial Park – move up around the axis to the second exit. (You can use your home vehicle.) You walk along the fence and turn right to find the entrance ahead. The fountain is inside, centered in the hall; to locate it, you need to walk past the core steles along the main avenue.

At the time of liberation and crisis, this was the largest cavern inside the planetoid, dug for the purpose of mining ore; but the mine became repurposed as a war memorial when independence was declared. The lights overhead fade out in response to your awareness and darken to a constant gray, reminding the visitor of generations past in the face of what is yet to be. With each moment, the baseline of your memories shifts, creating an unsettling dream atmosphere. The quiet, oblique space opens wide and resounds with your own breathing. You can touch the fragments and pebbles embedded in the stone mantle, but beware of your instinctive missteps – the ground is uneven. You can assert yourself and call from the inside, expecting deliverance, but any wrongs are products of your own mind and your preconceptions. You are the mirror.

Was: Blue Line to Memorial Park

The cavern inside you resounds with the purpose of generations past; you walk ahead, expecting the lights overhead to darken any second and the dream to fade out to the constant gray of baseline awareness. Turn to move, mine your memories for ore and liberation. You are here and with each moment you assert your independence, centered inside the planetoid you can call your own. You need to find the fence around the fountain, to walk along the main avenue and touch the steles; exit as the entrance opens wide – this is your need to locate your home when you are but a visitor, creating a memorial from repurposed fragments, the unsettling space inside became embedded in your core, reminding you of past missteps. Take up the mantle but beware the war, the instinctive response to right declared wrongs at the time of crisis – the quiet in the hall is the vehicle of your own uneven breathing and the ground shifts along an oblique axis. It is the deliverance of the mind – preconceptions dug in stone and atmosphere; the largest products mining can use are but pebbles in the face of what was – and can yet be. Mirror yourself.

Sonnet 65,000,000 BC

Mary A. Turzillo

Shall I compare thee to a dinosaur?
Thou art more suave, and less oviparous.
Rough bellows shook cretaceous glens of yore,
subduing prey for creatures more carnivorous.
Sometime too hot the breath of raptor steamed,
'fore Ice Age frosted cycad frond and tuft.
Thou'rt still alive, while dino's clock's been cleaned:
by meteor strike the sauropod's been snuffed.
Though featherbrained thou dost sometimes appear,
yet theropods are closer kin to birds
than thee, my own sweet mammal love. So, dear,
I'll praise thee not with roars, but clever words.
And, long as laser prints and cartridge toner's inked,
thou shalt not, as the T-Rex, go extinct.

Dark Matter, Dark Mind

Peter C. Venable

As galaxies outwardly swing,
The mystery mass is the thing:
They thought it was gravity
But all is a cavity—
So physics was left holding strings.

The Old Time Traveler's Song

William John Watkins

I like to sit and watch myself go by,
I chose the safety of the passing crowd
and though sometimes I try to catch my eye,
a nod, a smile, but nothing said out loud,

no word of warning, hint of coming joy
that otherwise might slip beneath the crush,
something beneath the notice of a boy
for whom the world is always in a rush,

an old man smiling with an absent nod
that might be meant for anyone or none,
an ordinary thing but slightly odd
a detail that might come back later on

years on perhaps, but still so sharp and strong
I'll know it marked the moment things went wrong.

[untitled]

Greer Woodward

Cthulhu partners

at the HallowEon Ball

tangled in tangos

Dare I Keep the Body

Stephanie M. Wytovich

The first time I saw a dead body, I wanted to keep it,
to hold it close and never let it out of my sight. It was
the most alive thing that I'd ever encountered and after
years of feeling stagnant, of feeling stuck, I finally came
back to life with the simple sight of his glazed-over eyes.
So I took him. I dragged him out to my car and placed his
corpse in my backseat and drove home as if it was just a pile of
groceries back there, as if it was a bad egg that soured the smell
and not the stench of his rotted flesh.

But then I couldn't leave him.
I wanted him with me everywhere I went, so I cut off one of
his thumbs and stuck it in my jacket pocket. I'd finger it
sometimes—scratch and pick at the nail when I got bored—but
then I wanted more of him with me, on me. I took a lock of his hair
and put it in my locket so it hung down next to my heart. I yanked out
one of his molars and sucked on the tooth when I missed his taste.
And when I really needed my fix, when I knew I couldn't be without
his touch all day, I'd sew a patch of his skin inside my bra
so I could feel him on me, always close, always near. It may
not have been a conventional romance, but our relationship thrived

until he withered away, decomposing like a banana peel in my backyard.
I buried him, along with my dirty secret, under the flowerbeds, and now
I smile every time I pick a rose. The girls in my office love them. They say
they bring the place back to life.

Eventually, You Become Immune

Stephanie M. Wytovich

At first it was only one cup a night. I'd boil the water
until the tea kettle screamed, pour it in my favorite red
mug, and test the temperature with the tip of my tongue.
Hot. Ouch. Ooh. I wanted it to burn, and it was only after
I couldn't taste anything that I threw in the herbs. I didn't
wait for them to bleed, didn't wait for them to clump together
so I could strain them out. No. I watched them hover on the
top like bloated bodies, and when they started to sink, I closed
my eyes and swallowed them whole.

And then it was two cups a night. Two cups of herbs,
two mouthfuls of bodies. I tried to change flavors
but I liked the way the spice and cloves rolled over my
senses and nipped at the back of my throat. So I made another
cup, this time, with even more herbs, more bodies. And
by the end of the night, I was drunk on death, bloated and face
down in the bathtub, my spirit overlooking over my corpse.

I shook my head and reached for the mug. Even now, I wanted
a steaming cup of bodies, but there weren't any herbs left in

the cupboards. No honeysuckle, rosebay, gelsemium. The hemlock
was empty. The jar for nightshade dry. Three cups of tea,
three mouthfuls of bodies. How had I survived that long?

Remembering Jean-Paul Sartre

Jeffrey Zable

I remember as children we played tag in front of his house
and even then he would say things like, "If I am it and I tag
you, it will still mean nothing. Even if I tagged you a million
times it would still mean nothing. Therefore I could tag you
or not tag you and in the end what is true is that nothingness
prevails, though being here means the game is us and we are
the game, which once we are gone will no longer be remembered
by you or me for the rest of eternity, if you know what I mean. . . .

Nothing Writes To Disk

Kythryne Aisling

Nothing writes to disk anymore—
the tumor corrupted the tree,
shredded and scattered the leaves.
So I capture scraps of data as best I can—
photographs, text files,
voice memos, reminders,
grocery lists, lists of lists, emails,
alarms to tell me to look
for the things I've forgotten.

They have an app for everything these days
but there is no synchronicity, no search;
I must leaf through the raw data
with my bare hands,
hoping to stumble across
just the right file
at just the right moment—
before I can no longer remember
what it is I am forgetting.

I keep religiously redundant backups now,
knowing all too well the fragility
of both technology and neurology.
I've already lost too much as it is.

I was eidetic once
once
but then the circuits shorted
wires crossed, fused
neurons misfired,
cells mutated,
pathways erased—

The checksums in my head
stopped working
a long time ago—
I knew what parity was,
a long time ago, once
but now it's all error codes,

404,
files not found,
please insert a startup disk—

So here I am with the future
in the palm of my hand—
"This is my brain," I say,
half joking, half apologetic,
knowing exactly how it looks—
another mother too caught up
in text messages and social media
to see her own son on the playground—
but spare me your pleas to disconnect,
because if I do, I will lose even more
than the moments you assume I'm missing.

Let me tell you about missing moments,
let me tell you about brain damage and the way
time stops
being linear, stops
being indexed, stops
writing to disk at all.
You try living with these gaps in your timeline,
and tell me how well you do
at staying in the moment.

So here I am on the playground,
holding the future in my hands—
trying to salvage something, anything,
anything of the past, of his childhood.
Write it down,
write it down,
write it down,
write it down
get it safely backed up
before the next hardware failure,
before the next cascade wipes out—
minutes? hours? months?

I never know how much I will lose,
just that data loss is inevitable,
the leaves will fall,
they always fall
the system will crash,
it always crashes
and I will forget, I will forget,
I will forget
that I have even forgotten.

Dearly Beloved

Mike Allen

andante maestoso
Long before the partiers arrive, the Arborists
form the ballroom, standing in a dolmen circle,
stretching their many arms until vine-fingers
meet and entwine, bloodflow causing all
their leaves to fan out in rosy canopy,
transparent teeth unsheathed in long smiles
that serve for windows.

allegretto con grazia
From opposite corners, they play
a game, a duet. Xora unfolds hir head
so its branches uncurl, fork heavenward,
a radial candelabra, inverse chandelier,
each stalk tipped with a gorgeous gold eye,
succulent fruit encircling light.
Danyel's neck, sleek and black,
stretches across the room, supporting
hir porcelain face. Ze winds hir neck
through the spires of Xora's cranium,
speaks to the rest through lips that don't move,
declaring hirself serpent in the tree,
calling for guesses as to which temptations
ze offers. A dance, someone chitters,
and X and D both kneel, elongated neck
that bridged the ballroom now a line
for us to limbo beneath. R tries first,
barely clears as ze bends sculpted legs
beneath hir custom body with its wings
and gables. The little dolls that hold
hir consciousness cheer from hir windows
as ze stands. F cheats, hir entire shape
unraveling in sea-snake tendrils
before ze undulates under the bar
in an hieroglyphic wave. We delight
in our clowning, how it rearranges us
through the room, each of us a work of art,
each random pattern a new curation.
M can't dance this game at all.
Ze towers above us, hir upper half
a stack of vertical diadem membranes
stretched over crossed bones, soaked

with shifting colors. Ze cannot flex
as we. Yet get hir out onto the plain
outside the Hierophant's city,
where ze can unspool all hir kites
from hir belly, let them swoop defiance
against the evergrey sky.

adagio
The gathered separate
into those with heads
and those without.
The headless more numerous,
their torsos replaced altogether
with cages of whistling,
musical bone, or deft
bonsai sculptures,
or miniature castles
populated by mechamenageries.
Those who've retained faces,
hewn more closely
to antiquated physiology
in their self-selected designs,
kneel ballroom center,
allow the headless
to place the maidenbox
restraints around them,
clamp them shut.
The prisoners bow their heads,
swivel gazes to the floor.
The headless dance,
weaving between them
in peacock display.
All are silent.
Only those few gluttons
for history can guess
at what the game means.

allegro con molto spirito
A whisper flitters ear to ear:
The Aesthetes are marching past.
D snakes hir head
to a windowsmile, confirms.
Even in this now
fashion has trends to defile.
The Aesthetes have all kept torsos,
disposed of their legs,
replaced them with outsized monkeybar skirts,

pyramid scaffolds two stories high,
their trunks crowning the points,
their unmodified arms outstretched.
Their tiny clones support their frames,
hordes of identical homunculi
marching beneath each one,
a laborphalanx of Atlases
holding up their parent bodies
on bulging shoulders.
They move forward in spirals.
Slow architectural dervishes.
Their discomfort is evident.
Deliberate.
It's true, M sings, peering through
the highest window. They've heads,
but no mouths or ears or eyes.
Now they all watch.
The Aesthetes believe, it's said,
existence without sleep or thought,
surrender to void and pain,
for long enough duration,
will inspire their bodies
of their own to birth
the next evolution
sans any surgery.
The partygoers silently will
this dream come true,
pray the moment arrives in front of them,
this spontaneous transcendence
something they all long to see.

Six Things the Owl Said

Megan Arkenberg

I.

I remember having roots.
I remember pushing my way, bare and raw,
    down into black soil cold as ice
    that never felt the kiss of sunlight
in places damp, heavy, sucking
in places dry and fragile as bones.
Men and women, passing above,
    touched my petals tenderly,

called me broom and meadowsweet,
sucked my scent like water
through thirsting nostrils.
But I knew little of petals. I knew earth.
I was roots.

II.

What is a flower without the earth?
A flower without the soil is a corpse.
To drink water through a rootless stem
is to suck through a slit green throat.
What are a thousand flower-corpses bound together
with string and enchantment, a gift for a lonely man?
A thousand dead flowers make a woman
and a beautiful woman makes a wife.

III.

A wife's body has three scents.
The first is the scent of meadowsweet,
of enchantment, hot wax, salt and musk,
of bare skin and soil sun-warmed.
The second is the scent of marriage,
of smoke beneath a thatched roof,
of running hounds, the bloody skins of deer,
of charring meat on an iron spit;
the scent that lifts its head at the sound
of a hunting horn, eyes wide, and daring to hope.
The third is the scent of earth
which only roots can smell.

Every man can smell the first.
Only two could smell the second.
And I alone know that the third is there,
deep and out of reach.

IV.

My husband thought he knew something of thresholds.
I cannot be killed indoors, nor out of doors.
Did he not know that flowers stems
have walls as thick as castles', that roots
have cells as close and safe as any convent?
I cannot be killed on horseback, nor on foot.
A flower's feet are in the air, our soft
and dancing petals; always moving,

turning with the world, we do not know
what it is to be at rest. Here,

I will tell you the meaning of my husband's death:
The riverbank is the water that sleeps
deep within the earth, and
only I have tasted it.
The bath is the water that a married woman drinks
through a slit throat.
        The billygoat is a husband who eats flowers.
And over all of this, the arch
that bears the thatched roof, watertight,
is the name "woman," which renders
your roots   invisible.

V.

Never trust in
        prophecies, spears, sows,
        eagles, enchantment, thresholds,
        husbands, lovers, or love.
But especially love.

VI.

I had almost reached the river when he caught me:
Father, father-in-law, wielder of string and enchantment.
He said to me: I will not kill you.
                I will make you
rootless,
winged.
        And I will give you a woman's eyes
too big and beautiful to look upon the sun.
        And I will give you a flower's tongue
that yearns for blood and rotting things.
        But never again will you touch the earth.
Never again will you taste
the dampness, the heaviness, the sucking soil.
The other birds, the worm-eaters,
will drive you up into the branches
and your feathers, like a thatched roof,
will cover you from the rain.
I will make you what a woman is
        when she is beautiful.

Winged.
Rootless.

100 Reasons to have Sex with an Alien

F.J. Bergmann

After *237 More Reasons to Have Sex*, by Denise Duhamel and Sandy McIntosh

1. More than one tentacle.
2. With suckers.
3. I mistook the blaster in his pocket for happiness.
4. He asked me what a being like me was doing on a planet like this.
5. His ventral cluster was magnified in the curved side of my rocket.
6. His ventral cluster was like a bouquet of blue flowers.
7. I said, "For me?"
8. He felt like a cross between astrakhan and curly endive.
9. I thought I was shaking his hand.
10. He thought he was stroking my prehensile appendage.
11. We both thought it was a diplomatic formality.
12. We thought we were responsible for the fates of our respective worlds.
13. I felt lonely because the universe was expanding.
14. I felt small because the universe was so vast.
15. I felt reassured because his presence meant we were not alone, after all.
16. The gravity field caused genital engorgement.
17. The anti-grav generator caused dizziness.
18. The solar wavelength triggered hormone production.
19. The Coriolis effect made my senses swirl.
20. Lit only by Cherenkov radiation, I still cast a spell.
21. Such unusual sex toys!
22. Which he referred to as "probes."
23. When he unfurled his wings to stretch, I thought it was a mating display.
24. I mistook his yawning for sexual arousal.
25. I mistook his indifference for sexual arousal.
26. I mistook his urgent need to micturate for sexual arousal.
27. He mistook my sneezing for sexual arousal.
28. He mistook my laughter for sexual arousal.
29. He mistook my sulking for sexual arousal.
30. He mistook my tattoos for a mating display.
31. My piercings were highly magnetic.
32. He thought my breasts were egg-sacs.
33. He said he didn't have DNA, so I didn't have to worry about pregnancy.

34. Parthenogenesis, on the other hand.
35. I had had it with humanity.
36. Not much else to do on an asteroid.
37. We were both too far from home.
38. The starlight was so ancient.
39. He said he'd let me fly his spaceship.
40. He said he'd let me play with his matter transmitter.
41. He said he'd let me play with his matter transmuter.
42. He said he'd let me play with his time machine.
43. He told me he was a divine messenger, and I believed him.
44. His silicon-based wings fanned my lust.
45. His pheromonal signature was intriguing.
46. His subvocal rumblings made me squirm rapturously.
47. His buzzing vocalizations gave me a migraine, so I closed my eyes.
48. Next thing I knew …
49. He didn't have a name to remember.
50. He looked nothing like my father.
51. He looked nothing like my ex.
52. He looked nothing like anything I'd ever seen before.
53. I was ripe for mischief.
54. The bubbles in his creamy center turned me on.
55. His outer integument was my favorite color, periwinkle.
56. His outer integument had a fishnet-stocking pattern, and those things really turn me on.
57. Including the seam up the back.
58. And 9-inch stiletto heels.
59. His emanations smelled like roast pork and cinnamon.
60. I was hungry.
61. I just wanted irregular sex.
62. I'd never done it in free fall.
63. He read my mind and knew exactly what I wanted.
64. A myriad of moonlets intensified my longing.
65. We were trying to establish each other's respective genders.
66. I told myself it was my duty as a Terran citizen.
67. I told myself it was my duty as a xenoanthropologist.
68. I told myself it was my duty as a xenolinguist.
69. I told myself it was the best available treatment for xenophobia.
70. We slowly climbed out of each other's Uncanny Valley.
71. He said he wanted to serve me.

72. He said he wanted to eat me.
73. He said he liked my "Cthulhu for President" t-shirt.
74. I was hoping someone would pay big money for the videos of our encounter.
75. Someone on *his* home world.
76. He said he'd take me on a trip aboard his magic swirling ship.
77. Which had a really cool hood ornament.
78. He said he'd take me 2,000 light years from home.
79. He said he'd set the controls for the heart of the sun.
80. He said his mother was a Space Lord.
81. He said he was a Time Lord.
82. He was way hotter than I expected.
83. I had a fetish for long striped scarves.
84. I had a fetish for the writhing of his ventral cluster.
85. And the plumes on his dorsal ridge.
86. His violet eyes turned me on. All fifteen of them.
87. He said he was a famous rock star on his planet.
88. He offered to let me make a plaster cast of his ventral cluster.
89. He said he was a famous artist on his planet.
90. He offered to show me his Rigelian-sandworm-excreta sculptures.
91. He said he was a famous poet on his planet.
92. I didn't believe him, but I didn't want to hurt his feelings.
93. He said he'd come all the way from Rigel just to hear *me* read *my* poetry.
94. He wanted me so much he put his space ship on autopilot.
95. He wanted me so much he didn't notice when we overshot our destination.
96. The stimulating vibration as our vessel entered the atmosphere.
97. I thought the ship would blow up any minute and this would be my last chance.
98. It was my last chance.
99. Our vessel was about to crash.

   The smoke of our burning intertwined and rose up toward the stars.

Sea Monster Objects to Term '*Kaiju*'

Robert Borski

So much is right in the article written about him,
from his uncensored opinion of the movie itself
("You mean *Pacific Rimjob*," he snorts), to his work
as a lay minister and amateur astronomer

("I've long been interested in certain movements
of the stars and how they affect estival cycles
of waking and dormancy"), that he's not sure
he wants to raise a ruckus. But in the end,
so disturbed is he by the constant use
of the pejorative *kaiju* that he winds up
taking pen in pod and begins to draft a response
to the editor of *Benthal Times*, opting,
at least initially, to distill his objections
to a few bullet points. Later, of course,
he'll try for something more eloquent
and maybe even personalize the final copy
with ink of his own making.

Point #1. Kaiju implies both a certain ethnicity
and place of origin. And while I have nothing
but respect for the myriad nations of Asia,
I clearly am neither of nor descended from them.
In fact, my haplotypes are *sui generis* and predate
even your earliest hominids. And while
convergence has given me a certain superficial
resemblance to members of local Teuthoidea,
most forensic genealogists believe my origin
is more stellar than oceanic.

Point #2. Unlike Gojira and his ilk I have
no aspirations to appear on the megascreens
of the world in eyepopping 3D and SurroundSound.
Narcissism and self-aggrandizement, with all
of its attendant woes (multiple marriages, groupie
sex, rehab, etc., etc.), are simply beyond my ken.
Seriously. Plus the last paparazzo who sought
to take a picture of me for one of your tabloid rags—
well, let's just say he probably would have preferred
to die from nitrogen narcosis and the bends
than what really happened to him.

Point #3 and perhaps my most salient objection:
your cities and population centers, enticing
though they be, do not interest me, and landfall,
with all of its ancillary havoc and decimation,
has never been part of my agenda. I'm far
more content to spend my days in this dark
pelagic realm I call home, thinking of ways
not to destroy you, but to *save you* through
my ministry. What *kaiju* has ever sought
that, hmmm? I defy you to name even one.

This, to summarize, is why, in reference to me
and my life's work, I continue to object
to the *k*-word.

Signed, *C.* (as I now call myself, since your spell-
checking software almost never gets my name right.)

Death of the Crossing Guard
Bruce Boston

The crossing guard
stands straight as a board
in the middle of the crosswalk,
his feet firmly planted
on the asphalt,
flush to the white line.

Dressed all in white
like an angel come to Earth,
he appears immaculate as
if he'd been photoshopped.

He raises the STOP SIGN
high over his head
in his right hand.
The onrushing stream
of cars and trucks
comes to a halt.

The children stream
across the crosswalk.
An endless stream of them
screaming as children do.
Walking backwards,
talking to friends,
making gestures and
laughing as lines
of children do
when they are let
free from school.

And then there are
the ones who walk alone,
heads bent and
eyes to the ground,
who secretly glance at

the growing stream of traffic,
wondering what it would
be like to sit behind
one of those wheels.

The line of waiting cars
grows longer and longer.
Some have started to honk.
Others rev their engines.
The crossing guard stands firm.

He switches the STOP SIGN
to his left hand and raises
it even higher, yet his shirt
is now stained by perspiration
and his posture has begun to sag.
Shifting uneasily from one
foot to the other, he looks
toward the end of the line
of streaming children.
But there is no end in sight.

The children continue
to stream across the crosswalk.
Screaming children.
Laughing children.
More and more children.

Until one car breaks free
from the pack and strikes
the crossing guard down.
And others in the endless
stream of traffic soon follow.

Una Canción de Keys

Lisa M. Bradley

Patricia, Nieta

My mother wouldn't understand
if I mailed her these cactus spines
smeared with blood,
mine.
My neighbor doesn't understand
when I bring her a cup of sugar
she hasn't asked for.

I say this as if I do understand,
but I don't.
I only know I want to give.
I want to offer up ...
something,
like a key on a kite string.

#

We buried my grandmother
with her keys.
A gentle joke at her expense:
she lived with iron bars
over her windows and doors
but worried she'd lose her keys
and die in a fire,
the house struck by lightning perhaps,
because we kids were heathens
who didn't go to church.
We pinned the keyring to her lapel
before we closed the coffin.
Now I think
that might have been a mistake.
If she wakes up,
she might come back home.

Emilio, Nieto

Where I grew up
you didn't borrow sugar from the neighbors.
You did learn how to unlock
a screen door from the outside
and the interior door with a bobbypin.
At least, I did.
But that was only for when I got locked out
of my own house,
I was told.
That was before I thought to ask
certain questions
("but how did *you* learn, Tía Ofelia?"),
before picket fences turned to chain link
and screen doors to iron gates.
The only thing that stayed the same:
the cactus stubborn as
the iron curlicues
guarding our doors and windows.
Prickly Pear, Stabby Sustenance:

nopales as second line
of home defense.

Patricia

We are a stubborn lot,
brigands and bootleggers and burglars,
burros all.
One generation of lowlife after another
though Mother managed to hide
our white-lightning past
til I was a teen.
We yelled a lot
happy or mad
at the table or across the house
and we all liked to be right.
"Ya ves?" we'd demand
when our omens came to pass,
the words rammed into one another.
Once we went legit
(in our eyes, at least)
we kept yelling but stopped
holding each other hostage
for validation.
"Llaves? Keys!" we'd tease.
"Yes, yes," we'd agree
to keep the peace, secretly chagrined
to be wrong, about anything.
Blue collar rather than black market
but stubborn burros still.

La Fantasma

I was buried with my keys
but now lie under oleander
my children put on my grave.
I could go home, but
why disturb the roots?
I have always loved plants
more than people.
Why go back
to those ungrateful brats?

Iliana, Nieta

Home was always Grandma's house,
even when it wasn't.

Once we rented a concrete house
with casement windows
and mats of Baby Sun Rose, not cactus,
flourishing beneath the crank-open glass
that often got stuck.
Iron bars didn't block our views,
only mosquito netting, because
this was still Texas:
Wasps and scorpions and tarantulas, oh my.

I loved the Baby Sun Rose.
Succulent but not spiny:
no good for nopales rellenos, but
maybe in a salad,
not that we ate salads.
Juicy, pink-flowered groundcover
so easy to take care of:
impervious to drought, indestructible.
It burst like blisters beneath our feet—
before storms we trampled it,
running around the house slamming
stuck windows shut—
but it always grew back.

It grew back as I watched two handymen
weld metal bars into the concrete windowsills.
None of us had proper visors
or even glasses, goggles, whatever.
I couldn't see the men's faces
through the afterburn on my retinas
but I sensed the pity in their gentle gestures,
the careful bubble of space
between them and me.

It grew back as Mother explained how to use
the stun gun
(I never asked where it came from)
though the cops had insisted
lightning wouldn't strike twice.

It grew back as I huddled in my room at night,
feeling watched, despite the curtains,
exposed, despite new iron screens.

I'd grip the black gun stock
and squeeze the trigger for 300 kilovolts
of crackling reassurance.
White fire filled the spark gap,
brightened my concrete bunker,
burned a Jacob's Ladder into my eyes.
I'd have lived in that box of lightning forever
if I could have.
But ... the batteries.
So I'd let go and, in the dark once more,
I held my breath, waiting
for thunder.

And outside the house that wasn't home,
the Baby Sun Rose grew back.

Reynaldo, Hijo

Burying Mom with her keys
was the last thing we all agreed on.
(The only?)

Over the fresh-turned soil,
Ofelia suggested oleander.
"You know how big those bushes get?" I said.
"So we'll have to trim them," she shot back.
"Yeah," Alma butted in. "At least that way
you'll pay your respects more than once a year,
Reynaldo."
Quietly, Evelyn said, "It's poisonous."
"Then it's a perfect match," snapped Hugo.
"What are you bitching about?" I said to him.
"You're not the one she whipped with a belt."
"No," he said, "I'm the one
who wiped her ass the last year."
We seethed in silence times five.
Six if you counted Mom.

"So," Ofelia finally said. "Oleander?"
Oleander.

#

I'm ... flummoxed ...
yes, that's the word,
when my sister Evelyn sends
her granddaughter,

mi sobrina nieta,
to my kitchen.

"Tío Reynaldo," Abigail says,
and girl looks so white, it's always a surprise
to hear the soft, quick T,
the well-rolled R.
But a *good* surprise, always.
"Evil Abuela told me
you'd help with this school project.
That'd you'd have recipes from Tatarabuela."

"Well, your great-grandma was kind of a half-a—"
I catch myself, but Abby grins.
"*Haphazard* cook," I amend.
"Must be where Mami gets it," Abby says,
and I pity my niece Iliana.
Evelyn, aka Evil Abuela,
should've sent that girl to me, too.

"Your great-grandma didn't write down recipes,"
I explain. "She really didn't have to,
made refried beans every day …"
I trail off, remembering soupy bland messes.
But we can't subject
Abby's classmates to that,
bad enough *we* had it breakfast, lunch,
and dinner. "But I do remember watching once
when she made nopales …"

"Cactus?" Abby shrieks.
"This isn't going to be like that weird salad, is it?"
"¡Cállate!" I say. Fucking Baby Sun Rose.
They will never let me live that down.
"Just trust me," I say. "Vas a ver."

(You'll see.)

A quick trip to la bodega—
the nearest one;
there are more in our neighborhood now
than when I grew up; as my husband says,
"Thank you, gentrification?"—
and we're set, not for nopales con huevo,
the slimy dish Mom made,
but a cheesy cheat better suited to Abby's palate:
nopales rellenos.

I'm unwrapping the newspaper-swaddled paddles
when a spine pierces my thumb;
the bodega clerk must've missed one.
It's a sharp key, stabbing into memory.
I suck my thumb to stop
Spanish curses from spurting out
but nothing can stem the flood of Mom
in my head, in my kitchen.

La Fantasmadre

"We called them *huaraches*," I tell Rey
as he and la niña place the paddles
in water dancing with onion, garlic and salt.
"¿No te acuerdas?
And there's no need to boil
if you buy the smaller ones."
He pretends not to hear,
but I know better, see his shoulders
pinched up around his ears.

When the paddles are tender,
he lets them cool, then shows her how
to butterfly them. "If you'd gotten nopal*itos*,"
I say, "that poor girl wouldn't have to handle a knife.
You could just sandwich the cheese
between two paddles with some toothpicks."

He snorts.
"This from the woman who used a machete
to slice everything
from onions to apples to raw beef,
without washing it in between!"

Reynaldo

"Now she's calling me 'hijo ingrato,'"
I tell Abby, who doesn't need me to translate,
thanks to her cousins,
Ofelia's wretched grandkids.
She rolls her eyes though, not quite sure
whether to believe me, as she hands over
the Oaxacan string cheese.

"You have three kinds of cheese
in your refrigerator," I repeat
for Abby's dubious benefit.

"You really had to go out and buy *this*?
And yes, I did. It's more authentic,"
I tell Mom and Abby.
And now Mom rolls her eyes. "Authentic?
Authentic's using what you already have."

She also has Opinions about
our dredging technique:
"You're wasting flour.
The batter will stick without it.
Three eggs is plenty."
But I spare Abby that.

When water drops shimmy and pop
atop the oil in the cast-iron skillet,
I let Abby lower the first huarache
and we both beam at the sizzle,
the crackle like benevolent lightning
in a pan. I think even Mom
is awed into silence by the beautiful browning
her great-granddaughter has achieved.

Then Mom mutters, "Don't let it burn, cabrón."

La Fantasmadre

¡Y qué milagro! No se quema.
I knew it—boy's queer.

Reynaldo

When Abby takes that first bite
of cactus spun to gold
crema and red salsa commingling on her tongue,
her eyes close and my mouth unlocks
our family's mantra:
"Ya ves? Llaves? Keys?"

Abigail, Biznieta

"Sí, sí, I see."
It sounds silly,
like a nursery song
or a jump-rope rhyme
but I don't care.
There's magic on my tongue,
alchemy,

new tastebuds rising
to the challenge,
completing unexpected circuits:
It's alive!

I open my eyes
and Tío's grinning like a mad scientist.

Behind him, a woman stands
with a slighter smile, like a door
just cracked open.
Pink petals in her steel-gray hair
and white light zigzagging
from the keys pinned to her lapel.

I wipe my mouth and rise to greet her.
"Bienvenido, bizabuela."
It sounds like another song.

"Gracias, querida," she whispers.

And Tío gasps as we await
the next verse.

Rule 44

Robert Payne Cabeen

If I could sing a love song,
I'd sing it soft and sweet,
Or maybe boozy-jazzy,
With a syncopated beat.
Or I could get real moody,
And sing it like it hurt.
My face would get all sweaty—
I'd wear a thousand-dollar shirt.
If I could sing a love song,
I'd tell you how I feel.
The words and the music
Would be beautiful and real.
The lyrics would be sensitive,
And everything would rhyme.
I'd write a haunting melody
And sing it perfect every time.

If I could sing a love song,
I'd sing it from the heart.

The depth of my emotions
Would tear you all apart.
I'd have lots of back-up singers
And I'd sing it really good.
I wish that I could do that,
But you know I never could.
It would be a violation
Of rule Forty-Four-B
That states androids can never sing—
And that applies to me.

They were quick to make us stronger,
Because they were so weak
And they even made us smarter
So we could think and speak.

They let us have emotions too—
From joy to deep despair.
They thought if we were like them,
We'd give them love and care.

But soon they sensed they'd gone too far
And did a heartless thing.
They passed android suppression laws
And now, I cannot sing.

There are so many, many things
I can and want to do,
But rule forty-four clearly states
I cannot sing for you.

I knew your secret whims and wants,
Obsessions, needs and fears,
That no meat-man could understand,
If he lived a thousand years.
On Earth, they talked behind our backs—
So hurtful, so obscene.
You knew it really bothered me
And said, "They're dumb and mean.
These small, small men, they envy you.
They grunt and snort and snore.
Their wives have robot boyfriends stashed
Inside their nightstand drawer."

Years ago, there were eager crowds
That cheered on blast off day.
Now, ships loiter above the Earth
And shyly slink away.

I long to hear those engines roar,
To feel the searing heat,
To see the fire, smell the smoke,
But now, that's obsolete.

Back then, starships had massive crews
Like sailors out at sea.
Our survey ship was self-contained—
With only you and me.

And what a perfect pair we were—
Victor-9 and Jolene.
We became the ideal union
Of woman and machine.

I loved your wit and confidence—
The softness of your touch.
When you smiled and called me baby,
I liked it very much.

When you went into suspension,
All I could do was think.
The lonely, lonely years crawled by—
No work, no food, no drink.

Out of ignorance or malice,
The makers never thought
To make a switch that would turn off
A robot astronaut.

My memories and fantasies
Were all I really had.
In that desperate isolation,
A human would go mad.

I once sat in your pilot's seat—
Consoles on either side.
My fingers ached to throw the switch:
Manual over-ride.

I feigned I was the captain of
A fast insurgent ship.
I swung a frightening gamma sword.
You cracked a laser whip.

We were cunning. We were ruthless.
We were bold. We were feared.
You wore a gleaming breastplate.
I had a thick black beard.

The bloated, sneering overlords
Would cry and gasp for breath.
As they made desperate promises,
You'd laugh and give them death.

The years slipped by, and you slept on,
Inside your chamber cold—
An alabaster effigy
That never did grow old.

I would watch your still perfection
All through your icy sleep
And drown in its complexity,
Your beauty was so deep.

When we got where we were going
And time for you to rise,
I would wake you from your slumber
And look into your eyes.

They sparkled and they shimmered when
The breath of life returned.
And when I felt your first heartbeat,
A fire in me burned.

When you sat up in your chamber,
You'd yawn and start to sweat,
Then toss your hair back with a grin
And say, "Are we there yet?"

I'd say, "I'm not sure where is there,
But this is where we are.
You've been sleeping for a long, long time—
Traveled very, very far.
Let's get some caffeine in your veins
And see what we can see."
You'd stretch and then you'd always say,
"I really gotta pee."

We were sent to find resources,
So they could make more stuff.
No matter how much wealth we found,
It never was enough.

We ventured further, faster—near
The speed of light we hurled,
Into the smothering nothingness.
We hopped from world to world.

At first you gave them noble names,
But soon grew bored with that,
Then named them after childhood friends—
You named one for your cat.
But there was wonder everywhere—
It seemed to fill the hole
That remained when you realized
You were not in control.

"Do the stars talk to you, baby?"
You said as far stars shone.
"I hear them whisper, now and then,
Above the engine's drone.
I try hard not to think about
The meaning of it all,"
You sighed and said, "But way out here,
I always feel so small."

We succeeded in our mission,
But you were not content.
Then deep inside Aquarius,
I knew what you had meant.

We passed the Helix Nebula,
Beyond all sight of land.
We gazed into the Eye of God.
You wept and squeezed my hand.

In time, we left our instruments,
Packed up inside the ship.
We tired of the flashing lights
And blip, blip, blip, blip, blip.
The universe is deaf and blind,
To every sight and sound,
But we became its eyes and ears—
So, we just roamed around.

We saw sights that brought us rapture
Heard sounds that brought us bliss.
There was awe and joy and wonder
Throughout the black abyss:
Colossal Clouds of gas and dust
Where infant stars are born.
Red giants in the throes of death,
With only us to mourn.

The stars, the stars—stars without end—
Burning, burning in the black.

What radiant astrology—
That cosmic zodiac.

And nebulas, like abstract art,
With colors bold and bright.
An artist would go mad with joy—
At such an awesome sight.

We found a regal, woeful world
Like we had never seen.
It slowly turned, alone, alone—
A solitary queen.

A ring of moons surrounded her—
A string of glowing pearls.
She wore a polar diadem—
Aurora rainbow swirls.
We strolled along the shoreline of
Her roiling sterile sea.
The diamond sand beneath our feet
Glittered mournfully.

As we moved on, you turned to me.
Your voice quavered and shook,
"Is there really any beauty
When there's no one there to look?"

It's true that science brought us here
And I'm its watch-work spawn,
But our mission seemed so pointless,
When all of them were gone.

We went beyond the black beyond,
Beyond stars with a name.
They'll never know the things we knew,
Or just how far we came.

I didn't have the guts or heart
To tell you to your face—
I was pretty sure that you were
The last one of your race.
What seemed like months and years to us,
On Earth, eons had passed.
Deep down, I always thought you knew
You might just be the last.

They're dead, all dead and dead again,
The ones who sent us here,

And their children's, children's, children—
And now, you too, my dear.

When oblivion came 'round for you,
You still were in your prime.
You missed all the indignities
That cruelly come with time.

How strange it was to cradle you
And gently stroke your hair,
To have you look at me with love,
When you weren't even there.
You'll live on in my memory—
Live on and on and more.
Across the star spilt Milky Way,
Alone, I will explore.

The makers gave me memory—
Because they soon forget.
So, I will long remember you—
Remember and regret.

If only there had been more time—
More moments to record.
So many marvels left unseen
And worlds left unexplored.

I returned you to the cosmos,
And I could hear the spheres
Whisper, "Come, my fragile creature,
Who was my eyes and ears.
Come drift until the end of time,
Where lonesome comets roam,
Through the endless canyons of the void,
That you had called your home."

Jolene, Jolene, Jolene, Jolene—
You echo in my mind.
That mantra takes me to the place
Where memories rewind.

I'll remember and remember—
You'll never wane away,
And when our story finds its end,
It always will replay.

And as it does, I'll tinker with
The makers' circuitry.

When everything that's them is gone—
What's left will all be me.

And when I find rule forty-four
The first thing I will do,
Is scan your cosmic sepulcher
And sing and sing for you.

The Perfect Library

David Clink

For Carolyn Clink
After Patrick O'Leary's The Perfect City

Imagine, if you will, a perfect library
where the reading room is lit by the soft
pulsing lights of fireflies & the wood that furnishes it
is from exquisite trees felled by mountain men
with bulging biceps.
Where you can find the fold-out book of universes
& newspapers including *The Barsoom Evening Post,*
The Fanciful Times of London, The Atlantis Monthly.
Where you can find dictionaries of made up words,
the histories and alternate histories
of things that never happened,
the book of extinctions & lost civilizations,
the book of the living, the book of the dead,
the book of the living dead.
Where the reference desk is staffed by ancient librarians
with leathery wings who can tell you about the Big Bang
& everything since because they were there.
A perfect library where the books read other books
& join book clubs, arguing what they're about,
& when they're done they shelve themselves.
Where you can find books smaller than a fingernail
& larger than a bus.
Where the listening room has pillow headphones
handed out by flapper girls sporting steampunk goggles
so you can hear the music mountains make,
the pent up frustration of dormant volcanoes,
the budding awareness of spring moss growing
on the sides of trees, the stirring of the planets.
The perfect library where documentaries are available
in a screening room with reclining bucket seats

& fresh-popped buttered popcorn & drinks are served
by male models wearing gladiator & toreador costumes.
Where the photocopiers never run out of toner,
paper, or patience & never break down.
Where the carpets are cleaned by pilot fish
taking a break from *Shark Week*. Where bathrooms
are hands free & faeries use the pressed leaves
from gilded books to fan your hands dry.
Where the map room has an infinite number of maps
& old sea serpents using walkers gingerly slip
from the canvasses to lead library tours.
Where the archives & special collections contain books
that have turned to dust & patrons are asked
to wear white gloves & to refrain from sneezing.
Where people in the quiet room can hear the building settle.
I have not mentioned the mermaid swing,
the petting zoo of extinct species, the corridors
where classic lines float through the air like balloon help,
the 2,000 Years of Cement exhibit,
the crystal conveyor belt made from the wishes of children
that appears out of mid-air, bringing the books you want,
the dungeon of dead technologies,
the wall of human existence,
the glass tube ride through the sunken city.
This is the library you dream about, the perfect library,
& I can see you want to go there,
you want to knock on its heavy oak doors & say, Let me in!
& if you finally find yourself there
you will discover the perfect place,
past the reading room of exquisite wood & fireflies,
past the guided tour, the swing, the dungeon,
past the gladiators & toreadors & flapper girls
to the place where you have a view on the garden,
the natural light finding its way in,
& there, in a glass case, you will find
the first library card you were issued,
the first book you signed out as a child,
& you are there with your parents again,
the place where you could barely see over the counter
& you are glad you finally have a chance to thank them
for taking you to your first library,
the perfect library,
& you realize, this is where you have been,
all along.

And I'll Dance With You Yet, My Darling

C.S.E. Cooney

Body, my darling
    For that time, age 11
        When I hated your big feet
        This nose I called blob
            The blobbiness in general
    For every zit demolished
        Cheap razor scrape
            For every bloody ankle
            I thank you

Body, my darling
    At 15, I thought you were God
        These breasts, God
            These hips he worshipped
            These hands, these lips and the subtle
                Tricks they learned
    Every ribbon in your hair
    Every bell on your bare ankle,
        Like a cathedral

Body, my darling
    At 6, you captained spaceship trees
        At 8, swam with mermaid feet, bound up
            In rubber diving rings
                At 9, rode your bike without training wheels
                In Cortez Park, crying a little
                    Bewildered but exhilarated
                    By mastery

Sometimes you dream of running
    The way others dream of flying
        I grieve to wake you, tethered
        To my strolling amble
            My pleasant pace that eats miles,
            But slowly

Body, my darling
    Any incline you see, you want to take
        Like the British took Bunker Hill
        You tremble at a sidewalk, want it rough
                    Right then
        Naked skin on baked cement
            Asphalt to untender callus

Glinting glass and ragged toenails
Entwined together, making of each other
A kind of summer

Body, my darling
You never did like your hair combed
And who can blame you?
There was always too much of it
Too much of you, us
Fraying so gloriously at the edges
And always, always tangled

We tend to overflow our waistlines
Eat to excess
Laugh like the thunder taught us
Back in our desert days
I thought it finer to laugh
Finer to love you
Than wallow in bitterness
But, oh, I meant to do better by you
Than this

I meant to teach you graces
Bravura to replace bravado
Leanness to underscore lavishness
A high cool gloss to finish you
Yes, I meant to make you cool

And I meant to dress you properly
Everything the best
But, Body, you refused
Flushing,
Crying you were too hot for clothes,
And won't I take you to the seashore
For dancing?

I cannot go, my Body, my beauty
With all the sorrow in me
I cannot take you dancing
Where just anyone can see

Know this, beloved
My source of inaction;
My love was made fragile by fear
By a jackass screaming
Out his rolled-down window
Reduced from personhood
By an egg shattering at our perfect ankles

I would not subject my enemy to such scorn

       Is it any wonder I must swagger you in secret?
       Keep rapier wit, written brow
          These ears, these eyes, these freckles
            This ulna, this ink stain
               Safe

And dance in darkness
   With only a thin silk of candlelight
   Between us.

Drawn to Marvel

Bryan D. Dietrich

Diagnosed diabetic the year I was born,
         You must begin with circles, some the size
my cousin taught me to live. How to let go
         of certain change, a dime, say, two quarters.
of a lit bottle rocket, pop the tarred, dark
         In the extremities, use even smaller ovals,
bubbles on days so hot the streets boiled, guide
         a geometry of diminishing returns.
go-carts, build robots. How to skate, stilt walk,
         As you move from one arc to the next,
clock a cropped horned toad with a rock, dodge that bright
         surprise yourself with lines, connecting
blood, what shot from its eyes. How to know a hero
         absence to absence until the frame
when you saw one, tri-colored, caped, omni-identitied.
         creates a trajectory of seeming
Late nights, lacklost in Lubbock, we'd saddle up the ghost
         action that almost looks like it could live.
cycle, thumb our way through Kung Fu, Daredevil,
         The hero you have begun—this stick figure
the man without fear, Doctor Fate, Tommy Tomorrow,
         fueled by long white, graphite, eraser stubble,
Spectre, Steel Sterling, man of steel, the New
         raggedy man made up of mostly empty
Gods, Kamandi, the last boy on earth.
         space—this imagined muscle vessel,
If it weren't for the diapers, ampoules of insulin
         well, he needs just that. Start with each

in the Frigidaire, you'd've never known. He lived
> *oblique, with the beauty of the gut.*
this way, in my memory, for years. Then suddenly
> *Continue with the pecs, making sure*
it's '82. They cut off his right leg. Dialysis begins
> *to look for where they connect. Don't leave*
seven years later. Three-hour hauls to the hospital,
> *his breast heavy only, unable to support*
three days a week, seven hours of recycling,
> *itself. Deltoid, bi-, tricep, the curdled*
new blood nearly every other day. The next year,
> *ripple of all you wish to appear,*
paralytic. Dead from the chest down. Still,
> *as they say, ripped … all this complex anatomy*
he can drive with hand controls, ride horses
> *may require help. Perhaps you should*
with a special saddle, keep his family believing
> *consult a book. If not, stop now, return*
by joking, popping wheelies in his chair.
> *where you started. Take off your clothes*
Then, three years before the end, bed bruises, skin grafts,
> *look at yourself, see how we all fit together.*
more than seven hundred stitches, arthritis, kidney
> *Bone, muscle, blood vessel, stubble, the subtle*
infection, colostomy, the other leg.
> *breaks between one undiscovered region*
A sore so deep it never heals. Later, the heart
> *and another. Finished? Time now for*
attacks, two of them. And hands … gone. Eyes, gone.
> *the face, the hair, shadow on the brow, under toes,*
Graduated drowning; his own humors. The day
> *other assorted endowments. Finally*
before he dies, strangers from Tombstone come
> *the costume. What you've been waiting for.*
to take him for a ride in a covered carriage.
> *This must be perfect, new, surprising,*
It is April—month the poets call cruel, flower
> *able to expand in every direction. He's a symbol,*
of the new millennium—when he finally says stop it,
> *don't forget. He must perform miracles, he must*
stop,
> *be brave.*
please,
> *Braver still when just*
just turn off
> *standing. He must abandon*

the machines
mere design, drawn to what marvel he was made for.

Spelling "For Worse"
Peg Duthie

When she saw the lettuce
tagged "for quick sale,"
she shuddered, recalling
her mother's forceful
forkfuls of salads:

"No daughter of mine
will fail
because of flab."

She no longer loves
the man her body won,
itself the prize
and still her prison.

Lacking the means
to leave, she starts
by sketching runes
on the walls of her tub
with each month's blood.

Then she begins
to cook for herself.
First, figs, poached in a wine
reeking more of treebark than grapes.
Watching the fruit swell up as it stews,
she whispers an alphabet of needles,
stabbing at clusters of hot-air compliments.

Next, olive puffs: cheese dough patted
around brine-slick beads. Lining them up
across the ungreased baking sheet,
she murmurs an alphabet of scissors,
snipping at purses and strands of paste.

Then she boils rice and molds it into brides.
Adding seaweed veils, she mumbles through
an alphabet of floods, blurring the grooms
off pages, off pillars, off pedestals.

Time for the walnuts. She blends them with cream
and pumps them into pastry horns. Stirring the glaze,
she quietly speaks an alphabet of flame,
whipping into ashes reins and apron-strings.

Hardened by neglect, the orange she seizes
isn't quite a relic, but its skin is tough and thin,
the juice unusually sharp. She plunges the flesh
into a syrup of cloves. As it steeps,
she sketches an alphabet of spurs in the steam,
redirecting parades and pageants.

She harvests rosebuds, rinses the petals,
and boils them into a jam. Rosemelt on toast.
Rosemelt on fish. Rosemelt straight on the tongue.
She swallows the sweetness before reciting
the alphabet of thorns. Her skin
is learning the gleam of scale and armor.

Sweetbread pie: a panful of organs
far more vital than muscle, yes? yet
sneered at for their pungency—
she drapes the crust without precision,
intent on mastering her alphabet of picks,
listening as the locks unclasp their links.

What's left? An egg. She spins it on her palm.
So many choices among her recipes.
Then she sets it down. The alphabet of shells
is singing to her of how a body's trappings
shine to the beached and the combers
once they catch the drift of shorelight.
The letters echo around the house
she's shedding even as she fills it.

Star Song

Kendall Evans

Forever together, you and I,
    We have occupied
        These vast
               & asteroid-blasted
      Forsaken plains
       for aeons

Do you remember eternity
        The long hard struggle
            Up from the sea
                    & taking our tea
                On the shoreline

Let us partake of the sacred blood
        The wafered flesh
                of the fallen brood
            While we discuss the conundrum
        Of what is real
                            & where we've come from

On that journey star-to-star
        You were the Captain
            I, avatar
                        In those dark
                & Time-dilated
                Far reaches

Or were you
                    The ship's A.I.
                        Dreaming In digital designs
            Ancient, wise--
                    You stroked my neurons;
            I was hard-wired

One of us will be
        A deity
                            The other diabolic
                & let's say you're singular
            The only one
                I will be legion
                    Far-star-wandering

Let us make love
            In the ruins of ancient
        alien civilizations
                    Allow our children to prowl
                        These haunted highways
                While howling
                at multiple moon-glow

We have gathered
                The sub-atomic grains
                Of galaxies
                    Navigated supernova
                    Nebulae

Let's have some fun
This eternity
          While we re-conquer the cosmos

House of Jaguar

Serena Fusek

• Couple

Behind overgrown briers
the condemned house
teeters on rotten foundations.
Light yellow as illness
sifts through dirty panes.
In one bedroom
the ghost of a white dress
rots from a hanger.

In the front room remain
a couch and a television
with a broken screen.
The jaguar reclines on the couch,
his spotted pelt blending
with the mildewed upholstery.
He rests his head on his paws
watches
the girl in the black slip
who sits beside him.
Through eyes like oiled stones
she watches a Mexican vampire flick
on the smashed TV
as she paints her nails
a pink bright as sunrise.
Is the scar on her cheek
that looks like a tear
a healed claw mark?

• Cat People

Briers braid knots
across the panes.

On the couch the girl
twines her legs into a lotus,
rests hands on her knees
circles pink thumbnail
to pink index nail,
stares inwardly.
The fragrances of an incense
called Rain Forests twists
into the odor of cannabis but
no smoke curls through the rooms.

On the TV that is plugged
into a dead wall socket
Simone Signoret
watches the caged panther pace,
her racing heart glittering
in her slit pupils.

The jaguar slinks in,
his bloody jaws gripping
the haunch of his kill.
He stretches out. The grinding
of tooth on bone scrapes
along the walls.

Slowly the girl's gaze
focuses on the feast. Her
jaw tightens. Smoothly
as a wave the cat rises
stalks behind the TV
swats the plug from the wall.
Simone lays her hand
on the cage's lock.
The girl disappears.

• The girl who lives in the jaguar's house

Her long bones slide
under translucent skin
the color of old book pages.
At her wrists,
thin as bird claws,
her blood smells of cinnamon.
Her hair shrieks in snarls

but her nails shine
the only color in the house.

Jaguar brings her
the rabbit's leg,
the tenderest bit of deer.
The house holds no fire.
She tears the meat into strips
with her square teeth,
swallows it raw.

• Great Red Paw

In the moonlight thorns
pattern the pane with lace.
The girl sleeps on the couch
her body fitting bonelessly
into its sags, her black slip
blending into its stains.
An old leak smears
wallpaper roses behind her.

On the floor the jaguar sprawls
on his back, his paw—
soft as a cub's around the claws—
curled over the pale rosettes
on his belly.

On the broken screen
painted singers twitch without sound.
The girl's lashes flutter,
a mewl escapes her throat.
The paper roses ripple.
The smear flares like a
flower opening   spreads;
darkness tinged with scarlet flows
down the wall. The sharp stink
of meat enters the room.

The jaguar rolls over,
flexes his paws.
Two green fires spark in the dark.
He pads behind the couch
his tongue dips into

the red flood rasps
along the plaster.

• Living in the house of jaguar

In the Mayan language
one word means *meat eater*:
jaguar. In his eyes' slit pupils
she sees portals to the dark latitudes
the night sun travels to morning.
When his breath falls on
her flesh she smells
the death of deer,
the sweetness of mint.

She can glimpse his golden sleekness
only in the corner of her vision;

if she looks at him straight on
the energy in his atoms seethes
like yellow jackets swarming carrion
until he flames with the fires of Hiroshima.
His weight lying on her bones
pushes her hips
into the couch springs.

• Fly away home

Through fog glittering
on the TV screen
Bela Lugosi's white-rimmed eyes
rake the form of a fainting blonde.
The girl crouches on the couch,
chin on her knee that
she strokes with a long nail
on which pink polish chips.
She has not seen the jaguar
for two days, not since
the wall leaked blood.
Her body trembles until
her teeth click, but as
the sun warms the room
she unknots   steps one

bare foot to the floor
tiptoes to the door.
In the sallow sun draining
through the door's glass
briers knot ironwork patterns.
She slides along the hall wall
but when she reaches the stairs
she sprints. Dust rises as she runs.
She pulls the filthy slip from her flesh,
tosses it over the banister.

Upstairs she peers
into each empty room.
In the front bedroom
in clean light through
a window free of thorns
the white dress glows.
She unhooks it from the hanger
pulls it on. Age has thinned
the fabric; the knobs of her bones
shine through.

She struggles with the window,
cracks her knuckles
against crumbling sash.
It crashes open. She climbs
to the porch roof, picks
her way across broken shingles
to the edge, spreads
her arms, kicks off
into golden air.

• Condemned

The shovel clanks over curb;
tires roll over waist-high weeds
a predator could hide in.
The grass falls and the machine
stops. The driver jumps down,
strides to the condemned house.
The briers that climb its siding
have bloomed: four-petaled roses
white as a bride's gown,
silky as her flesh.

When he touches one
perfume seeps along his senses
like rain-forest smoke.
He pulls on a glove,
pushes through the thorns,
peers into a window. Inside
a couch collapses into the floor
before a TV gray as ashes
in a grate. Then, on torn pillows
he glimpses a flash of gold,
two amber stars
staring at him.

He blinks. On flimsy floor
only ruined furniture.

He climbs back on the shovel,
yanks a lever.
Metal sinks into dry rot
that cracks like bone shattering.
Walls, struts, nails
tear away screeching
like a woman or
an angry cat.

Row Your Boat Ashore

Adele Gardner

For my father

Last night, I learned, you took your final breath
About the time I woke and worried
You had slipped away. No phone call, so all's well:
But the heart knows, somehow. That week before
You went to hospital, my chest was tight
With panic that all time had slipped away:
And yet I didn't call, I didn't stop by, didn't stop
Typing your words long enough to hear you speak to me—
I'd held that fear so long, though never so strong—
I felt I couldn't breathe. You tried and failed,
An oxygen mask for life-vest, vent for raft
Kept you afloat till we could swim to you,
My brother catching me just as I left shore,
Pushing off for your house, our weekly visit.

He steered me to hospital instead of home,
Your final stop on earth.
                                    We waited, parched,
Thirsting for your words, your breath,
Hanging on that little sound—mechanical, loud,
But regular, as numbers monitored your fate.
You slept. We stroked your head, held hands
That gripped us sometimes as you rose from sleep,
Head cresting for that sip of air, one eye
Peering for us through that distorting, liquid surface
Of pain-meds and sedation. You floated, drifting there,
Effortless in sleep, but struggling when they demanded
That you consciously stroke the waves by yourself,
Stay buoyant on the strength of your own air.
You were tiring, eyes scanning for us, for shore.

We tried to lift you up, hold your head above water,
Hands stroking forehead, hands, arms,
Loving, encouraging words, our voices a beacon
That might call you back. We praised your every breath.
The breathing trials went better when we stood beside,
Each of your swollen hands gripping ours,
As we prayed and told our love, to make your spirit light,
Help lift your burden and smooth you over the waves.
It worked enough that we began to hope.
They took you off the ventilator. Mom called us for goodbye,
Then brought your glasses. You saw us clearly through still water:
You held out your arms, hugged my brother
Like a man clinging to a spar, his hope, his strength.
But your hoarse breath filled the room, four times as fast as ours,
And we anxiously gulped each minute,
Afraid they'd not add up to hours.
So much pain, and yet you fought for us, for each breath,
Gripping our hands so tight
It was clear you were saving us, not the reverse.

We were drowning, holding our breath, our eyes flooding
As we felt your pain rasping with each shallow, rapid breath,
So much effort, to lift one chest—
Far more than you needed to crush our hands with love,
Hold us in shaking arms. You brought our hands together in a cross—
My brother and I, then our entire clan—
Clear symbol we must stick together,
Keep this boat in one piece—each other, afloat—
This family ark you'd built with each patient breath
Over so many years.
                                    Stroking your sweating, swollen brow,

Sister says you should think of the calming lake,
Our favorite place—imagine yourself floating there,
Peaceful, easy. Relax, try to nap,
As you did on the cool porch to the sound of waves.
You're slipping away from us, stealing away from shore,
The current carrying you out to the end of your tether—
But you will not let go, your grip stronger than ever
As the waves shake and rock you,
Your breath jagged, monstrous waves on the computer graph,
Your heart racing to keep up.

                                 I'd give anything
For one more breath, one more word.
Your eyes, the squeeze of your hand
Are all I have to translate. Poet, dreamer, pragmatist,
You often used concrete symbols to make your point:
I think of all those people you taught to swim: my brothers and sister,
Aunts, uncles, cousins, me: the way you cupped my head in one big hand,
The other just under my back, your soothing voice
Telling me to relax, don't fear the water,
Just breathe. I wanted to thrash, splash, get my feet
On the lake's stones: but you held me, and I held still.
We floated, daughter and Daddy, who was the world.

I search your face for the words you can't say, panic stopping me
From saying anything that might suggest your end.
You keep your eyes on us, so large and moist, looking frightened,
Uncertain for the first time, no lenses to shield and sharpen,
Straining to catch us through the blur
Like an exile squinting for each last glimpse of home,
The land dwindling as you put out to sea—a line, a point, gone.
Where are you, under that starry sky? I'll guide your raft.
Swimming through night after day,
I fear my lungs will find their own watery grave
If you let go. Brother talks to you in the darkness,
Telling his children's day, small points of color
Glowing along the shore. At last visiting hours end.
I don't want to go. I keep looking back.
Mom sleeps beside you in her chair. At last
You slip your moorings, push off,
And quietly drift away from shore,
Eyes on her sleeping face, her own breath serene while yours
Rasps like the snore that guarded us so many years.
One last time, you row through night-lake waters,
Black and smooth as silk—dark as the night she swam,
Trying to decide on your proposal,
Till you swam out fearing for her life,

And found her calmly dripping
On the shore of your love. Time stops,
The ticks of your breath silenced. They close your eyes.
But you're already out to sea.

Hollow Beats the Night

Delbert R. Gardner

December blew white tracers past the window,
And somewhere, children would be building snowmen,
Dreaming of the time when Santa Claus
Would prop up Christmas trees with stacks of gifts.
Though Nelson Strong was scarcely forty-five,
With dark brown hair as yet untouched by gray,
And lithe-appearing body used to movement,
He sat each evening in a trance-like manner,
Refusing to take part in conversation,
And stared with hollow eyes at nothing earthly.
Some friends came, after hearing of his illness,
And tried to cheer him up with apt remarks,
Like "Don't kid me, you're only tired of working,"
Or "May, how long you going to pamper him?
I wish my wife would wait on me like that."
But, getting only curt one-word replies,
Unsettled by his pale, unwinking stare,
They fidgeted, already sensing Death,
Afraid to stand inhaling His black air.
They fumbled their goodnights and quickly left;
May walked them to the door and softly wept.
"Poor Nelson, I don't know just how to help him.
For three weeks, ever since the doctor told him
That any kind of labor'd stop his heart,
He's sat and looked like that, and never eats
More than a bite or two of food, that's all
He ever eats. I don't know what to do."
They tried to comfort her, in awkward kindness;
"This thing has kind of thrown him for a loss,
But he'll perk up within a week or two,
You'll see," they said with hope they did not feel.

The children had been always close to Nelson,
And now they could not understand his quiet.
"Your father needs his rest," May gently told them.
"He isn't well, and we must all be patient.

Let's give him all the help and love we can
And pray to God to give him back his health."
Lucille, at twelve, was eldest of the three.
She sat upon the floor by Nelson's chair
And, smiling, put her hand upon his knee.
"What would you like to get for Christmas, Daddy?"
Tenderness was throbbing in her words.
He looked at first as though he hadn't heard;
And when he turned his head to look at her,
His eyes were prisms of his bitter soul.
"Death," he hissed; then, seeing how the word
Had struck her in the face with freezing shock,
He briefly touched her hand and said more gently,
"I just don't want to be here Christmas Day."
She put her face upon his knees and sobbed,
"Please don't say that, Daddy, please don't die!"
Her younger brothers stood by looking helpless,
Not understanding why Lucille was crying,
But close to tears themselves in sympathy.
May hurried in and pulled Lucille upright,
Caressing her to soothe the wracking sobs.
The man stood up and threw his wife a look.
"If you don't keep those kids away, I'll kill 'em,"
He muttered, and walked slowly to his bedroom,
Shutting the door upon his daughter's wailing.

Lying in the darkness, Nelson listened
To the uneven hoof-beats of his heart;
"Useless-failure-useless," it insisted,
"You almost got your wish, your wish to die;
Just one more crisis, one more strain like that—
I'll end the farce, and stop cold, stop you cold."
"Oh, no you won't," said Nelson, "not that way;
I want it slower and more natural-looking.
Besides, if you won't work, I'll starve you!
No work, no food," he said and chuckled lightly.

How long he slept he had no way of knowing;
The house was lying under heavy silence,
As he became aware that some intruder
Now shared the darkness that before was his.
"Who's there?" he whispered hoarsely to the room.
A soft, soft voice came floating through the gloom.
"You're frightened, son. It's only me, your Mother."

"It can't be—but it sounds like Mother's voice—"
Then, suddenly he knew it *was* his mother;

His being was pervaded by a calm,
A quietness he hadn't known for years,
And nothing seemed unnatural or strange.
Silent and unquestioning, he waited.
"I want you to go back to sleep and dream,"
His mother said. "I want you to remember,
And be again, a boy of twelve years old.
Goodnight, my son, sleep well and don't forget
That every man must be a child first."
The mind of Nelson swiftly bridged the years
To that hot summer when his mother lay
So near the reaching hand of hungry Death,
That every breath he feared would be her last.

> In the close and tiny bedroom,
> Nelson sat beside his mother.
> With a cardboard fan, he fanned her,
> Through the hot and sticky night,
> Dozing seconds at a time,
> Till her gasping "Fan me, fan me!"
> Brought him guiltily awake,
> Made him fan with freshened vigor,
> Saying underneath his breath
> "Get well, Mother, please get well,"
> Praying hard as he knew how,
> "Save her, God, please make her well;
> I won't ask for nothing else."
> Once she felt a little better,
> Looked at him with loving eyes;
> "You're so tired, dear," she said,
> "Go to bed and get some rest."
> "No," he said, "I'm gonna stay."
> Smiling then, she fell asleep.
> Nelson went and ate a sandwich,
> Fixed some beef broth for his mother,
> And fed it to her when she woke.
> Morning brought the scorching sun,
> Making the bedroom like an oven.
> Not a breath of air was stirring
> To relieve the stifling heat.
> Nelson's mother gasped for breath,
> Begged her son to keep on fanning.
> All that day he waved the cardboard,
> Changing hands when one went numb,
> Wishing that some rain would come,
> Wishing that the day would end.

Evening finally chased the sun,
But the air was thick as ever,
Sticky air too hot for breathing.
"Let me get a doctor, Mother."
"I've no money for a doctor."
Nelson's mother wrote a note.
"Take it to the little church,
Where we used to go last spring.
Give the minister the note;
Ask them all to pray for me."
Saying this, she lay back panting.
Nelson was afraid to leave her.
"Hurry, son," his mother begged him,
"I'll be all right while you're gone."
Kissing her, he hurried out,
Buckled on his roller skates,
Skated as he never had,
Jumping curbs and broken sidewalk,
And the clicking of the wheels
Matched the pounding of his heart.
Tears were blurring in his eyes,
Causing him to pass a street
Where he should have made a turn;
Soon he was completely lost.
Frantically, he dashed around,
One direction, then another.
Desperation mounted in him,
And his breath was coming short.
Then his eye fell on a sign
With "M.D." behind the name.
Knowing that the sign meant "doctor,"
Nelson stood before the house,
Wrestling with his indecision,
Till his worry for his mother
Overcame his fear and shame.
Quickly taking off his skates,
Dashing to the porch and knocking,
He asked God to help his mother,
Make the doctor help his mother.
After what seemed endless hours,
Someone came and let him in.
Pushing past the skirted figure,
"Where's the doctor?" he demanded.
"Doctor Williamson is busy."
"What's the trouble out here, Thelma?"
Asked the doctor, coming forward.

Nelson ran to kneel before him,
Threw his arms around his legs,
Begging him to help his mother,
Saying that they had no money,
But he'd work and pay him back.
"She's so sick, I know she'll die,
If someone don't come and help her."
Dr. Williamson was touched;
Maybe he could see himself
In the mother-loving boy.
"Thelma, bring my bag," he called.
"Come along, son, you can show me
Where your mother and you live."
Nelson said he had to find
The little church somewhere around there.
"Come, I'll take you," said the doctor.

Getting out before the church,
Nelson humbly thanked the doctor,
Told him where his mother lived,
Begging him to go ahead.
Going in the little church,
Nelson hurried to the altar,
Gave the minister the note,
And kneeling down, he prayed out loud,
Asking God to save his mother,
Get the doctor there in time,
Help the doctor make her well.
Everybody listened to him,
Feeling shamed before his faith.
When he ran back up the aisle,
"Pass the plate for that boy's mother!"
Shouted someone in the back,
And the preacher stood amazed,
Seeing four plates overflowing,
Emptied out and filled again.

Nelson paused before the bedroom,
Hardly daring to go in.
Then he turned the knob and entered,
Saw the doctor standing there,
Saw his mother, pale and quiet,
Breathing softly in her sleep.
Dr. Williamson was smiling,
Leading Nelson out the door.
"She'll get well, my boy," he said.
Nelson's knees began to shake.

Sinking down upon his cot,
With his face between his hands,
"Thank you, God," he mumbled weakly.
Looking at the boy, the doctor
Mixed a glass of medicine.
"Here, drink this," he kindly ordered.
Nelson gulped the bitter fluid,
Then he settled back and slept …

When Nelson woke, he looked around the room.
Daylight slanted through the curtained window,
And May was dozing in a chair beside him,
Her head against the back, fatigue lines showing
Around her eyes and mouth. Humility
Began to spread its balm throughout his soul,
Crowding out the bitter, useless feeling.
As if she felt his loving glance upon her,
She gave a start and looked at him with fear,
But when she saw his open eyes, she smiled.
"Feeling any better, dear?" she asked.
He nodded. "Better, but I'm awful hungry."
Surprise gave way to gladness in her face.
"I'll fix some breakfast for us both," she said.

He ate with such a relish it amazed her.
When he was done, he looked at her and asked,
"What day is it?" "It's Sunday," she replied.
He hesitated, wondering how to say it.
"Mother was here on Friday night," he said.
She nodded slowly as she gazed at him.
"I think I'd like to see the children, May."
Her eyes were searching. "I'll go get them, Nelson."
Lucille came in with reddened nose and eyes,
Followed by young Fred and Nelson Jr.,
And May was smiling at the door behind them.
He solemnly shook hands with both the boys,
Then, hugging his daughter close, he kissed her hair.
"You're what I want for Christmas," he said gruffly.

The Alchemy

Neile Graham

De Sphaera: Lib. I, Georgij Bucanani, translated by I. C.

The tymes of light & shade, Turnes heat to Colde,
And sunne & moone with darkenes doth enfolde,

spark a match to the wick. Light the dark.
This is the small apocalypse we live
each day, our cells dying as we build
ourselves anew. Open the book. Inside it:
black on near-white. Scrawl sprawling, crawling.
Twisting into shapes, growing limbs. Figures,
tree-tall, which become intent. Someone's will
to pass a message to the future. Me. You.

What sounde, what murmur, thinck you, will resounde
Whil'st the whole Earthe doth walke her hasty rounde,
And all her woodes, rockes, hills so high that ryse
Shall rende the aer: who can expresse the cryes?

Shouts and yells. Screams. Shrieks. Yelps.
Roars. This language I don't know how to begin
to read. How to be brave enough to sound out
the graceful, furious gestures cedar branches
etch on the air. The words made of scars
of the wind's passage, of the scent of snow:
at first the world's new sparkling skin,
then the choking blanket thinning to rags
to mud in the starvling days before
anything dares to grow.

All this thou seest arounde, beneathe, above,
With endelesse motion Tyme's softe wheeles to moue
All Comprehending

of the distant memory of lightning, of want,
of storm, of soil propping the breath
of a seedling, giants sharing sun and rain
to let their sapling grow. Compete, compete—
Concentration shapes them. Words
build the cedars which pass their messages
hand to hand through what seems like nothing
(remember the void?) but never is. What seems
like something is something still. The empty air
the moment before it's dense with rain.

This night sky flashing with light,
the silence thunder fills.

In this vault are thrust
Fower all compounding bodyes: Earth the firste,
Then water, on whose face the fleete aer flyes,
Then lightest fire, next to the azure Skyes.

This is what I'm saying now. This is what I say to you.
Night is not a small thing. Nor is what we light against it.
These words beneath those forest trees.
Huddled there: someone, anyone, I see you now
and the message you receive: Let the other hungers
give their voice. And in the silence
they all speak (remember the void).

Leaue then for shame, your frantique appetite,
My soule bidds speake.

Speak anew.

Roman Shade

April Grant

Dedicated to Faye Ringel

Prologue

A summer evening at Aunt Celie's house:
She entertained the Poet and myself.
He wore gold rims. I thought the world of him.
Celie, the social lioness, in search
Of plum and melon ice cream, tactfully
Stepped out and let me show the Poet round.
Rooms of sea-green, peach, silver, dull gold, blue,
Antique and vintage, lacquer, marble, glass.
Our Poet ambled through it in his tweeds,
Approving this or that with little nods.
He smiled upon the paintings, busts, and prints,
The views of Edo and the Russian vase,
And Celie's grand piano, cream and gold.
On all he beamed, and in his beams I basked,
Watching his lips for brilliance. "What's in here?"
The darkened dining room we never used.
The Poet murmured, "Ah! Yes! Roman shade,

Remarkable." I couldn't stop to ask;
Ideas came flooding fast. I stood and guessed.

1. She-Wolf

In the height of summer, smoke goes up from Rome.
Beneath the fig tree, their mother lies and pants,
Her flanks heaving. In the shade, she smells sacrifice.
The tyranny of sun glares white from those walls;
Her sons grew alien, and left her to her grove,
Went off to be day creatures. They were both soft.
They were smooth and chubby, could not bear nipping,
Learned to walk clinging to her angular sides,
Clamped their mouths on her dugs, as real cubs would do.
Hundreds of years have passed since then. The she-wolf
Many a time has borne cubs of her own flesh.
She loves them. But she never forgets the weak ones.
They must both have mates by now, and cubs of cubs.
When they grow old, as she, eternal, will not,
They will have children to lick their faces clean
And hunt for them. The she-wolf is comforted.
She never saw the wall her human boys built.
By that time they had both forgotten her milk,
When the naked wolf-lad leapt over the wall.

2. Arena

I grew up, grace-given, under the stars striding;
I slew the lean lion and the deer felled daily,
They caught and bound me, as the brown bear mighty,
In chains they bore me from my cliffs of hunting.
Here in the caverns of Rome am I cabined,
In builded blocks' darkness, as a cur cowers.
From here they will hoist me to most hateful sunlight,
An oval plain, shadeless, eyes over eyes staring,
Friendless, to force men at my spearhead to stagger,
Till one drag me downward to meet shadows' mercy.

3. In His Habit As He Lived

"I'll meet thee at Philippi," the ghost sighed,
Looming above the youth of aspect sad,
Who squinted at the specter and replied,
"I thought you were supposed to be my dad."

"But aren't you Brutus?" said the Roman shade.
"You've come to the wrong theater," said the prince.

"I hope you find him." Caesar, much dismayed,
Vanished with fog and an embarrassed wince.

4. Antique Roman

In that same castle by the sea,
Much later, in another room,
While lamp wicks smother in the gloom,
Blood's cooling on the marble floor.

Beside a pile of noble dead
They've known their whole lives long, there lie
Two students. One came home to die.
The dark one holds the fair one's head.

The drugs to put him out of pain
Stand by the dark lad on the floor.
He'll follow after; he is more
An antique Roman than a Dane,

And there is yet some liquor here.
The fair boy, lying on his back,
Slaps down the glass to roll and crack,
With the last strength of his career.

Somebody has to stay behind
To see their story still draws breath.
"Mine is the easy part, that's death.
The labor's living, as you find,

To live's the hardest task of all."
The fair-haired boy begins to fade,
He whispers, sighing out his shade.
At last there's silence in the hall.

5. Mount Auburn Cemetery

H. Wadsworth Longfellow, I've heard it said,
Lowell and Holmes,
Lie in Mount Auburn's hills of mighty dead,
Where now the tourist roams.

I, with my guidebook, and a friend in tow,
Too awed to talk,
Passed by the marble houses, row on row,
And fought the urge to knock.

Up a long hillside, under hemlock trees,
Tombs faced a brook.

Every door had a window with a grille.
I meant to have a look.

The first was dark to my sun-dazzled eyes.
Something had groped
With muddy little hands at the next door.
Just a raccoon, I hoped.

And next, a tomb's screen door, like iron lace,
A dark design.
Deep in that tomb, a grimly smiling face
Was staring into mine.

The honesty for which I'm always known
Leads me to say
I fell back flailing, gave a strangled moan,
Leapt up and ran away.

A cooler head prevailed. That ancient shade
Inside the tomb
Had been as white as marble. Less afraid,
We faced him through the gloom.

That eagle-nosed and grimly smiling face
Far at the back
Under a skylight, in a sunny place,
Stood out against the black.

Was he the image of a man who lay
Near in a box?
Was he a prank meant for a sunny day,
To give the tourists shocks?

Was he, perhaps, some rich collector's prize
Among the dead?
We whispered, "Ave, ave," to the eyes
Of that white, knowing head.

6. In the Roman Wing

Free day at the museum:
I walk from bust to bust,
Among the marble Romans
Collecting clean dry dust.

Dead eyes in beaky profiles,
Old men with baggy skin,
A bull-necked man of action,
A widow's dimpled chin.

I paused before a matron
Of curly, braided head,
Her eyebrows raised, disdainful,
And this is what she said:

"Slaves with a saffron awning
Would keep me from the sun;
Both modest and accomplished,
I worked in wools and spun.

"Hairdressers I had seven,
And half a dozen maids,
The envy of the City,
Girl masters of their trades.

"I beat them when they failed me
Or when they made too free.
I bore no man's reproaches:
They all belonged to me.

"Now sold and caged in crystal,
To all my face is bare,
While children suck their fingers
And old plebeians stare.

"Slaves with red hair disheveled
Pass by me but to say:
'Oh, is that Cleopatra?'
And then they walk away.

"My ancestors about me,
I'd thought to take my place,
To watch my children's children
Burn myrrh before my face.

"Base animals! Why bear me
To bondage, where I fade?
Oh, let me sink in darkness,
Delightful Roman shade!"

7. The Old Women

M. Aemilius Structus, junior secretary to the Governor, to his wife Cornelia.

You need not fear, my plum, I have abandoned you.
That I have failed to write may be ascribed to the state.
Tonight, I'll make one letter do the work of four.

Here you may meet the fabled brutes in dirty furs
Who bathe three times a year and grow their shaggy beards,

Who heard no Latin till they were fully grown,
Pursuing feuds in vengeance upon their neighbors' cows.
Their neighbors' women and children suffer most.

They lament at their new Governor,
Who will not let them play their little games of blood.
Of course they loved old Sica, who,
Having gone native, lay unwashed upon fur rugs,
A lover at each hand. They try our patience.
The Governor is quite as vexed, but hides it well.

We must remember they are children,
These huge and dirty fellows. Only little boys
With the powers of men. One can't expect a child
To thank you for a thrashing, be it never so deserved.
You know that just as I do, mother of my sons.

You need not fear a rival. Let me say it once again:
The thought of a barbarian with watery blue eyes
Holds no appeal for me. As for the brutes,
One never sees their women, and sometimes I think
Barbarians are solely men, who breed by sprouts and buds,
Or spring from horsehairs dropped in mud, as serpents do.
We suffer presently from childish spite. Three days ago
One of them leapt upon and stabbed a legionary.
(We've set a guard upon the temple of Minerva;
These creatures will pry off the roof tiles, otherwise—
They do not count it theft to steal from Romans.)

The poor guard, Laenas, never out of Rome before these hills,
Will lose an eye. He killed the leaper, who was very old.
So ugly and so old a hill-man I have never seen—
They murder one another in their middle years,
For the most part, before they can achieve gray hairs.
He was naked, and about his neck hung certain stones with holes.

We could not find his knife, and I vow that is a nuisance,
Since those animals say Laenas struck the first blow.
Otherwise, they are deaf. Often these days I wish
My time was out and I was tossed by whirlwinds to your bed,
My tiny mouse. I wish this three times a day.

The only touch of beauty in these hills occurs at dusk;
The dirty swine all cook their meat on open fires outdoors.
Their flames shine near and far. When they're too far to make a
stench,
Why, one might think a hail of stars had showered to the earth,
Although their drumming spoils the peace. You'd find this a fair sight,

My dearest plum—and this alone, of all sights here.

We finished off the fish sauce weeks ago, and now
We have no way to kill the taste of hill provisions.
One may eat even rancid lamb if one enlists the help
Of fish sauce. We are almost through the wine. By the fifteenth,
The mule train should have reached us. We are counting days.

Today, we held the trial. The Governor made up his mind
To rule that Laenas commited manslaughter,
And must pay blood price to the dead man's dirty kin.
Though this humiliates the lad, still, his centurion
Stands with us: we have not only to be just,
But to show Roman justice done before the demi-men.

It falls to me to find descendants of the ancient beast.
They say he has no kin left, but they're lying out of spite.
They're inbred, brother-cousins, nephew-sons, bred back.
He must have kin. And so I spent today out getting nosebleeds,
Battered by the windstorm as I trudged between their huts.

I brought an officer and men along
In case of trouble. I looked into goatish faces
That said "Not me," or feigned to speak no Latin anymore.
They traced their toes in patterns on the dirt. At times
I wonder why we try. Golden Apollo could descend,
Singing of Troy, and they would bite his arm and hump his leg.

The day begins to fade. A man can sit beside the lamp,
And write, as I do now, and sip his wine in twilight here,
Content and almost happy. One forgets the dirt and flies
And hill-men. This half-measure is the last wine I will see
For Bacchus knows how long, so I had better make it last.

As I began this letter, came another wretched fuss:
A naked little boy ran up and shouted at the legionaries,
All in that gobbling tongue. Still, there was one who understood—
A half-breed, though it's not his fault—he says the boy cried out,
We will release the old women,
We will send down the old women upon you.

Of all the threats I've known, that's feeblest.
What harm will they do us, will they spin us to death?
But, no; they are barbarians, no one here spins.
I'm picturing their hags, freed from kennels, with disheveled hair,
Crawling along the earth to bite us with their toothless gums.

Crawling along the earth. It's curious. I almost wrote,
"A cloud has snuffed the stars," but clouds have veiled the sky all night.

The stars upon the land, the hill-men's fires, are going out
In swaths, and the most distant hills are wholly sunk to night.
There is no sound. It's drawing towards us in a wave.
Blackness is putting out the stars of fire.

* Epilogue

I ceased, and, for the first time, was aware
Of Celie trying hard to catch my eye.
The Poet had been shifting where he stood,
As though to speak. The sun had slid around
Until it glowed in through the golden silk.
"Were any of my guesses right?" I asked.
"What's Roman shade?" That made the Poet blink.
"A shade, of course! Why, that's a Roman shade."
He pointed at the window and its blinds.
"When the Victorians tried painting Rome,"
Said Celie, "they gave Caesar drapes like these.
But, still: good guess." "Oh. Thanks. My throat is sore."
"That ice cream should be nice and soft by now.
Let's go eat," said Aunt Celie. So we did.

Mining Planet

John Grey

Some planet this.
All that remains are dusty flowers,
sere lakes, decapitated mountains,
derricks, windlasses,
the many holes of giant moles,
some overeager machinery
already burning holes in next year's ice.
And the giant gray prison of course,
guards in grizzled gray,
cells full of rag-tag petty criminals,
well beyond their withered rap sheets,
some political lightweights
futilely scratching manifestos on steel walls,
and a few counting down to their execution.
Lastly, the warden in his glass-domed aerie,
a fiberglass desk of malevolent faces...who lives? who dies?

And in tiny town,
a basket of withered fences and prefab houses,

some poplars cased in translucent metals,
street lamps bearing away the coffin day,
night cracking open the number three hundred in neon
above a face in the window, making no sound,
a hundred lives in the head calling it home.
Another house, in clay askew,
a woman in a tin suit
has cried for seventeen years.
Her husband's dead, son in jail,
and the prison death-squad hot seat
buzzes in anticipation.
Like death itself, on a constellation stallion,
in rides the yellow-gray moon.
Then fitful sleep, another dream
of throwing herself at the executioner's feet.

On to the Galaxy Bar
where pensioned-off empire builders
battle scruffy young turks
for the right to be the most beast in man,
tattooed arms, roaring tongues,
and battered heads
where somewhere gets lost in nowhere.
Midnight moves in for its piece of the bloody action.
A black pall covers all,
The holy man of all faiths
almost choked on his last prayer,
has grown fond of mocking God,
besides, he figures, he's light years
beyond His fiefdom anyhow.
Backwater religious life's all tinkling censer,
busted Bible pads, croaked Koran,
sagging pews, tattered Torahs,
and a Hindu deity with more heads than followers.
Father, cry the voices from the houses:
There's a woman, and she has sinned
There's a man, and he's alone.
A harsh wind is all that answers the call.
He's the silent standard-bearer
for a stone-deaf religion.

Headquarters:
Bad news from the mines:
the ore is almost tapped out.
How long before mines close,
executions are fast-forwarded,
executives go home with their platinum packages,

miners take their cancers elsewhere,
the drunks, the hopeless, scratch their heads,
wonder where everybody's gone?
Even the rats are counting down the days.

Saline to Atlantis

Herb Kauderer

For David Livingstone Clink

I wanna tell you about Chlöe Hall
not the woman of rumor
the real woman
the woman of fact.

Chlöe lived for salt
drank extra sodium Diet Pepsi at every meal
covered salt bagels with salted butter
ate ham in kimmelwick rolls
baked salt pork coated with pumpkin seeds.

Chlöe sweated through the doctoral program
at Johns Hopkins University
by keeping to herself & studying hard.
She relaxed by playing in the ocean
& diving into the music of Celine Dion.
She graduated with highest honors.

Dutifully she crystallized her career
in genetic engineering
hiding her salt lust
abstaining through lunch meetings
keeping her vice submerged
until 15 years later she emerged from the
R & D elevator
at the top floor of her field
where she took the last
brave bold step
out
of her closet to become

a social pariah
worse than Madonna at Buckingham Palace
worse than Mike Glicksohn at a temperance rally,
worse than Patrick Stewart at the Hair Club for Men.

At company parties
fashionable up & coming executives
fled without decorum
as she shook salt onto pate
sprinkled cayenne sauce on caviar
crushed saltine crackers into lobster bisque
& chased it all down
with flagons of Diet Pepsi.

Oblivious to her talent
top geneticists fled the company
to escape Chlöe's saline insanity
& she was crushed like road salt.
Her economic triumph dissolved by social disaster
like a pillar of salt in a monsoon.
By the time her dry season returned
her resolve precipitated out
from the pools of social rejection
like the tracks from an elephant's tears
as it makes a forced death march
across the desert.

In her first year out of the closet
just to prove she could do it,
Chlöe created water-breathing mice.
Salt-water breathing mice.

In year two she made
water-breathing cats
because every mouse
must have his cat.

And since every dog must have his dog paddle,
she created phosphorescent ocean-living seadogs.

In her 15th year of resolve Chlöe perfected
Homo oceanus
& 6 years later she perfected
the genetic realignment procedures
that allowed land-bound wannabees
to follow Chlöe's personal migration
to the world's newest economic superpower
the prospering coral towers of Atlantis.

In her 29th year of resolve, and
her 68th year of life
Chlöe decided to outdo Mary Shelley
and attempted to create the perfect

salt-loving ocean-dwelling life mate.
But she failed & died trying
died an outcast
died childless & alone
in her coral laboratory.

I wanna tell you about Chlöe Hall
who was mother to us all.
Her salt lust birthed *Homo oceanus*
Her sandpapered heart constructed
the saline express to the depths.

Chlöe died unloved & alone in a country
that owed her everything. So I want to ask
you all now to shed a tear for Chlöe Hall.

Pay a tribute of saline
to the architect of Atlantis.

Words Not Red

Herb Kauderer

A cycle of cinquains for Geoff Landis

Outside
we ventured to
approach the pedestal,
men walking the crowd of monsters,
hidden

by our
audacity
as we surged to hear the
fat & jolly poets. They spoke
of the

moment,
dedicated
to the conquest of space.
Military conquest. They spoke
of those

lost, the
dead people in
their heads who live on in
asteroids & memorials

named for

them. They
abused all the
undecipherable
poetry of rockets & space,
turned red

with blood
ideology
exponentially
spread by the persuasion of those
speaking.

That was
the night I left
the city of fat and
jolly poets determined to
escape

words as
deadly as a
pulsating machine gun.
That was my good fortune as the
night burned,

and well
into the next
day the city was too
hot to enter. The city has
cooled and

I look
forward to the
rebuilding, this time with
poets thin & grim, using words
not red.

Said Rapunzel to the Wolf

Sally Rosen Kindred

1.

You should have been in my story.
I'd have been one of twelve daughters.
My story has sisters. Those sisters had hair
the color of moons. Their beds circled mine

nights in a stone room
that anchored our sleep. On hard ground,
iron as your eyes. We had no need
for a ladder: we got to lie down

and stay down. We got to rise
into song, shared words that curled
on our skin.
But the room had a door

and there is always a witch standing there.
She's Mother:
one thing my mouth can't change.

2.

My story starts in the throat.
The throat is a tower: the story climbs out
of that red cage, personal, burning,

crawling in cinders along the grass
until it climbs
your hackles, your gray ruff.

My story rides you out of here
across the bridge to a forest
where the witch can't pass.

Not to meet the prince.
It wants to be alone
with you.

My story wants time
feeling your breath heat
its fine hair.

You are wild. You throw us off,
my body and story. But I know you hear.
You're fierce.
You will bear us.

3.

Safe in the woods, but we've forgotten
those sisters. We must return
for them

which means finding
their dresses torn
in the starry brambles. You'll carry me,

lay me down to weep at their empty shoes.
Sisters: it was a mistake to make them.
Just lost girls. Something else we can't keep.

4.

You belonged with me.
I had the greater need.
I had no red hood, nothing to cover my head.
Truth? I had no sisters to cut the hair

from me before
it could be mounted.

5.

What was worse
than her casting me into your woods to die
was how, betrayed, she cut
my hair, as if

the real daughter nested there,
as if the dead blond sheen of me mattered more—

how she held to it, held it
to her cheeks, crooning
when I was no longer on the other end.

At once, I could see
my prince would do the same.

Nights now, blind to other beauties,
he reaches for my neck's lost cloud, longs
for it to grow
and give him back

his reason for climbing.

And she
starves in the tower,
satisfied to have it,

the long braid of some other girl's song.

6.

My story cried out for a wolf.
Stop panting. You could have come
at any time.

You could have been its sorrow,
its graveyard, its animal rage,
the moon's gray back

I drove across the cornflowers —
or the teeth I needed
swinging down.

I would have let you be afraid.
We'd move together, a body,
a new breath
named
by fur and blood: no mother's knife,
no golden stair.

Encounter While Waiting for Transport

David C. Kopaska-Merkel & W. Gregory Stewart

"For real adventure
you can't just mess around with kid stuff:
wormholes
subspace
star-shot time travel
cryogenics
swapping genes"
   he said,
   then spun this tale of
   climbing out of one bubble universe,
   somehow dancing across the continuum
   in which they're all embedded,
   and slipping down a hole into another,
   like in *The Magician's Nephew.*

   (Holes in this part of Creation
   (if you go in for Creation,
   or the panMythicConcordance,
   if that
   or else
   Holes in this part of
   Just What it IS)
   do a choke-neck spiral down
   to a pointparticleimpossibility
   or a piece of String …)

I thought he was going to say something
about how he came from
another universe
much cooler than this one
and I was going to
wonder out loud (but only just) why he ever left it
and be all DEFENSIVE
about my paltry three dimensions
but
he interrupted my interruption
like he had some kind of
temporal fugue going
or maybe he was just firing
on a better class of brane cylinder

"... feet up to yer ankles
in quantum foam and your head
stuck in one dimension of a Calabi-Yau quandary
while you wrap your ass around
the Far Horizons
of the first 3 dimensions
and wait for your table in the 4th
which is ALWAYS late
when you don't tip the maitre d' enough, well,
or anything ..."

blah blah blah.
(there are only 11 ways to die,
and only one of these has anything to do
with Einstein at a distance -
the rest are Darwinian somehow -
but here's the thing about a multiverse
spawning infinite sub-verses at any/every
point o' choice—
it was invented by dweebs who comfort themselves
with the thought
that even though they don't get the girl
in this life, they can still kick sand
back somewhere else.)

but of course this is not what he meant:

"There's something about a Brane transplant
and I've got a case of
surebellums so alien it's not funny
in my transport and well you see
I've got to move them
before the Expiration Date

(two months from last
Wednesday by your reckoning
but almost 3 years ago by mine)
and this Irish fellow
runs the bar out by the spaceport
he tells me
you might be interested
or know someone who is."

   I am about ready
   to show him the bum's rush
   because I've heard this story
   plenty of times
   on planets a lot more
   sophisticated than this,
   when he pulls out a sample
   and I have to admit
   it's like nothing I've ever seen:
   ticking
   wild paint job
   and what looks like
   a V8 or better
   under the hood

   so I've got a portable
   with me and we
   jack the thing into it …
   … now, there are some places,
   some planets,
   that just scare you the second
   you see 'em.
   there are sounds
   that take you back to bad times
   and smells...
   you see where I am going with this.

   this was every place like that
   and every sound and every smell
   and oh! I did gag most emphatically

   and he laughs,

"There now, and didn't I tell you?
That's a Hell in a handbasket, isn't it!?
Get over it, man, and LOOK.
Would you look at the thing?"

and this is something I did try to do,
to look

"There in the wet places, there
in the dark. Do you see? At the shore,
do you see? At the edges,
where the tiny gods go to die
where the primary mumbles 'dawn'
from time to time. There, do you see..."

   ... and I suppose I did see,
   or I did begin to see,
   while every twitching part of me
   cried to be blind or drunk or both.
   both, best, actually, and all this
   after 37 seconds,
   so I yank the jack and grab the Jack
   and pour a shot and hand it back
   and empty the bottle and stare.

and stare...

   ... until I don't care where he came from
   and I'm about to tell him
   just what he can do with his
   toxic alien brain furniture
   and I'm making a note
   copying it to my symbiote
   to stay away from this particular
   waystation the next time
   I have to kill time
   on this sorry orb
   that's way too close
   to the edge of everything

and way too far from anything that
spells Home:
  nucleic-acid based life
  instant food
  mass-produced entertainment
  robot-made garments with familiar logos
  conspecific sexual partners

Numbers

Mary Soon Lee

*Later, a historian, striving for the appearance of candor, said he couldn't determine
precisely how many people the demon burnt in their towns, but that, by using the most
meticulous methods, he estimated between 16,020 and 16,150 perished thus.*

*Seeking the authority of precision, the historian next stated that 18,272 men,
16,164 women, and 4,769 children followed the demon to his island fortress and there
served him in dubious ways.*

When the demon died,
fewer than two thousand
of his servants remained alive
within his fortress.

He had not hoarded his human treasure,
but spent it, singly or by the dozen,
setting servants aflame
in the dining hall.

Fewer than two thousand left
when King Xau came,
yet still the number
seemed overwhelming—

people lay collapsed in chambers,
passages, stairwells;
inert, parched, many injured,
all dying of thirst.

*The same historian, a soured and stunted specimen, dismissed King Xau's part in a
peevish paragraph. He said that doubtless the king visited the fortress, but that the king
himself saved no one, merely ordered his soldiers to wake the dazed sufferers.*

The king's soldiers tried
to rouse the survivors;
the sailors who had brought
the king to the island tried:

they could not rouse
one man, woman, child.
Instead they wet the sufferers' lips
(most swallowed, some did not),

and took them to the king—
who did not look kingly
(a fact the historian would have reported
gleefully had he guessed it).

Xau slouched, slovenly, sweat-soaked
over body after body;
his hands on chest, face, neck;
speaking, whispering, croaking.

Five died before the king
had time to help them.
Thirteen more (injured, weak)
woke, but died within days.

A few of the survivors
achieved distinction:
the glassblower from Angshan
rose to the head of his guild;

the china bowls made by one
female potter were hailed
(over a century later)
as the greatest of their age;

thirty-two men enlisted in the army,
of whom one became a captain of note.
Most returned, their names unrecorded
by history, to ordinary lives.

Curiously, when they remembered
the king kneeling over them,
each recalled a heroic figure:
young, handsome, clean, richly dressed.

Many described him as crowned,
the crowns as various as the speakers—
plain or jeweled, arched or unarched,
gold or silver or iron.

Only the soldier who carried the king
back to the ship accurately remembered
the man in his arms: smelly, shaking,
stammering, crownless but a king.

The Matter of the Horses

Mary Soon Lee

General Qiang stood in King Xau's tent
with the king's other generals
and the king's advisors

and the king's guards
and the king's serving boy
and the king himself,
the tent crowded with men,
rank with sweat.

The young king sat on a stool,
his left arm in a sling,
a grimness about him
that matched Qiang's own mood
though the war was over,
the victory theirs,
the king's advisors jubilant.

Qiang hadn't slept last night.
Had tried to sleep. Failed.
Yesterday's battle still with him.
The horses. Mud, rain, blood.

In the tent, the talk moved
to the matter of the horses,
to how it could be exploited
for conquest.

"No," said the king.
One word enough to quiet the tent.
"We do not crave conquest."

"Even so," said an advisor,
"we should test the limits
of your control over the horses,
the better to employ it for defense."

The advisor turned to Qiang.
"General, how would you proceed?"

Qiang looked at the advisor,
a man who'd never fought a single battle,
who'd sheltered in a tent yesterday,
warm and dry,
while rain cascaded from Qiang's saddle, his armor,
turning earth and horse-shit to stinking mud,
Qiang riding on the king's right
(the king, injured, unable to hold a shield,
but still riding),
Qiang's horse maneuvering beneath him
before he even gave the commands,
all the horses in perfect unison
as if they were a thousand shadows

of a single faultless form—
a thing out of legend,
out of the old times
when dragons flew to King Nariz
and demons walked the earth—
the stench,
the pounding of hooves, of Qiang's pulse,
as he rode beside the king,
as the enemy charged full at them—

And stopped.

Every horse in the Red King's army
rooted to the spot
though their riders kicked them.
Whereupon the Red King,
red-haired and red-handed in war,
screamed in his barbarous language.
And then the enemy had slaughtered
their own horses,
slitting their necks,
the horses foundering in blood–

Qiang looked at the advisor and said,
"If it were my decision,
I wouldn't test the horses.
I would let them be."

"Even if inaction now leads to defeat later?"

"Even then."

Into the stretching silence,
the king spoke:
"What happened with the horses
is not a trick to practice and parade,
but a gift. A gift the horses gave.
A gift for which many of them died."

The king's gaze rested on Qiang, anchoring him.

Qiang touched his hand to his heart,
offered it palm-up to the king,
a gesture Qiang had never made before,
the sign of allegiance of warriors
in the old tales.

The tent crowded with men,
but for that moment
only the two of them.

The Virgin and the Unicorn

Mary Soon Lee

He preferred boys to girls:
mud-footed, grubby boys,
who caught fish bare-handed
and dammed the stream with rocks.

He watched in silence
from a stone's throw away,
his coat the color of reeds,
his mane a shifting shadow

as he studied the bruises
on one boy's face
before allowing his coat
to lighten to silver—

the boy's intake of breath,
hesitant fingers on his mane,
and then their first ride
under a sea of stars.

Which is what he remembered
two summers later,
when the boy, snotty-nosed,
weeping, begged him not to go—

not to a stupid girl,
that it was a trap:
that they wanted his horn
to heal the king—

"I know," he said, flaring
his nostrils and breathing in
the scent of the boy,
"I know, but he's my king too."

*

Not the fairest,
nor the youngest,
nor the cleverest
of the King's daughters,

but the only one
to offer help

when he lay fevered,
his flesh soiled, his breath stinking.

He, the King, ruler of all
within five days' ride;
he who once tamed wild horses;
he who rocked her in her crib.

For him, she stood by the lake
on Midsummer Eve,
a battle-sword clutched
in her two-handed grip.

First the grass stirred.
Then came a smell
like the first jasmine
in the first spring,

then a sideways eye,
starlit, watching,
and a voice: "Unless you sit,
how do I put my head in your lap?"

In her throat
the taste of the sea.
"My father. The King. He's dying.
They say your horn—"

"I know. I came.
But, tactically,
shouldn't you have tried
for a surprise attack?"

The unicorn stepped forward,
his breath cool against her,
that smell of jasmine again
when she raised the sword.

Braiding

Sandi Leibowitz

The stolen ghost of you,
mute stand-in,
your shirt hangs white in the closet
wearing only its red-thread wounds,

thornless roses I once stitched
so you would guess I loved you

The scarlet flower that bloomed above your heart
looks like a bull's-eye, I realize
before I cut the knot that keeps it whole

Fingers deft as Penelope's,
I unpick a single thread,
unwhorl it, dedicate it like honed blade
to my devotions,

unbind my hair
Dark curls slip to my shoulders
like heavy serpents

Two long strands I pluck,
lay them alongside the red thread,
straighten them for the rite ahead,
witchery of hope
—love's purpose requires at least
the fallacy of smoothness—

pull the scarlet filament
taut as bowstring,

and begin to braid,
binding you to me

This act is not without cost,
no love ever is
It's not just our joys that join

I take unto me your wounds,
know soon I will kneel
with silver cup to catch the blood
where others' arrows lodge
as you will staunch my torn flesh,
staining your white cloths red

Once I wielded a silver knife,
        Soul-Skinner,
sharp as neglect,
its hilt incised with words
of love and praise withheld
For each lover, I slashed off
some scrap of my soul
till she limped, misshapen
queen of rags

But I have tossed away
my knife, renounced
diminishment.

Now I braid
life to life,
knotting your heart to mine,
singing a song
of addition, completion.

I am Ariadne reeling in her hero
towards the labyrinth's core
where he will soon embrace
her brother-self, that shaggy
rag-furred minotaur

The final knot is tied
Loose threads are one
This love cannot be undone

See in the shadows
the queen of rags enlarges,
dancing,
the red thread round her neck
incandescent as a string of rubies
or a rope of lies.

The Santa Claus Triptych

Sandra J. Lindow

Santa Claus is not material;
every child knows, he is
anti-material, allowing him
to change shape and fit
down chimneys, held together
by an artificial gravity mechanism
that also separates him
from toys he holds
in his other dimensional knapsack.
Everything is very scientific
and on the up and up, literally,
no fuzzy fantasies here.

The Polar Plausibility Theorem
maintains that when
e = energy and t = toys,

a something less than infinite
x weight of t can be transported
transglobally in 24 hours,
despite atmospheric conditionals:
various combinations
of wind and freezing H_2O
—low temperatures
actually facilitating
the superconductivity process.

Deconstruction:
Late one night recently,
on a trial run,
over Wisconsin,
Santa was testing
new antigravity gyros.
Needing to adjust his seatbelt
to make room for fluctuating
girth, he removed
his antimatter containment glove
and it fell from the sleigh,
taking out a trio of old dorms
on a UW campus,
temporarily being used
as faculty offices.
The buildings,
reminiscent of Moscow in the '60s,
dissolved and slipped into a lake,
hastening a peregrination
they had been glacially
taking for the last forty years.
Residuals of the anti-matter effect
removed noisome algae and pollution,
leaving the lake pristine.
No one was harmed,
but a hundred de-officed professors
presently sit in lawn chairs
around the deconstruction
arguing how to explain the event.
Any child could tell them,
but they haven't asked.

Butterfly Effect

John C. Mannone

For Vidya

If prayers are the pleasant
scent of flowers, then butterflies
must drift with its nectar, lifting
it up to Him.

A friend asked me about prayer.
Told me how it didn't work for her
and that even the null hypothesis
worked better. She said,

forget faith, just pray.
But to whom, I mused, the Fates?
I suppose, Hollywood would
agree with that mythology.

Horrible things happen
to good people, while louses
revel in injustices. I know.
After I was robbed

so many times, I wondered
if my God was out
to lunch when I called on Him
to protect me and my home.

I had faith, but was it waning
as a pale moth?

Just about the time
I was about to give up,
I heard a loud *rap, rap, rap*
on my door. I jumped

out of bed … another bad dream:
punks with bats and guns.

#

A preacher on the radio
started teaching about Job.
Yeh, yeh, yeh, I said, *I know.*
That poor schmuck

lost everything and got sick
as hell on top of that.

His "friends" said Job didn't
have faith or that maybe he pissed
God off. He believed them,
until God showed up—

a voice in a whirlwind,
but at first he might have thought
the whoosh was from his own
labored susurrations. You'd think

God would've told him
why. Instead, He talked

about the awesome
truth of nature, His creation,
and who controls it. It wasn't
Job; he remained speechless.

God didn't tell him about
the deal with the devil, or how
that scoundrel challenged God
to test his loyal servant.

But in the end, Job was restored
and where his sores had been
a butterfly landed.

#

Once my plane iced up flying into
unforecast icing conditions: had to
made an emergency instrument approach.
It was below minimums.

Yet He cleared a path at the last second,
at my last prayer.

Before I knew The Christ,
I had faith—I believed in the Father.
And He reminded me of it. I have faith,
but is it fading? No, it is not,

I have metamorphosed into
a monarch.

#

Pray with the innocence
of a child? Do not worry

about the wicked people
for they will be changed

as the fat dripping into flames,
only wisps of soot remain.
Don't worry

about the healing of your body,
it is done the moment you ask,
whether on this side of heaven
or the other.

If you ask Him for something,
how do you know that prayer
doesn't bump into another
someone else had asked?

We are all connected,

like the wind, and our prayer
gossamers the air. A butterfly
on a solitary lily flutters for just
one impatient moment.

How could it know
that later, in the next
season, across the sea,
it might have stirred

a funnel wind?
          So too with prayers.

Some are unanswered now, perhaps
to avoid a conflict of interest,
or chaos others might have to endure.
How would we ever know?

Perhaps the answer to our prayer
should best be delayed.

          #

The purple Twilight hoped
the night wouldn't come,
prayed the Daylight to stay. But
Darkness drifted in anyway.

The stars glistened as tears
which it couldn't even wipe.
Why? Why didn't you stay,
it asked. And the Day said,

I must bring the light to your
brother, for he is in darkness.
Yet I will return, I promise.

Enjoy the luna-moth moon
in the meantime.

Then Twilight's sister, Dawn,
brought the hope of Day.
And, as if it had forgotten,
Twilight would soon pray
again.

But one day, there will be
Light all around, and Dark
will have to flee forever.

#

Almost 3000 years ago,
because of their faith,
three young Jews were thrown
into a fiery furnace

with a fire seven times hotter
than hell. And they prayed while
rejoicing in their resignation,
but the Lord saved them.

Almost 30 days ago,
a prisoner on Death Row
found Jesus, even in the privacy of his
own hell. Before the execution,

he prayed as Daniel did the night
before. He had painted placid lions
on a wall. When asked what if
he wouldn't be saved from death,

he pointed to another wall
he painted: Elijah in his fiery chariot
meeting the Lord in the clouds,
he said, "just in case my ride

is with the needle."
Yes, they pushed it into his vein.
You could tell that he was not alone
by the shimmer the doctor later saw

in his eyes—a glitter of gold light
like a myriad of miniature butterflies

fluttering their metal wings in the sun,
a light that must have been at the end

of the tunnel where He was waiting:
the One who's already prayed
for us all, the One who suffered
the turbulence of our sins.

Does this help me understand
why that child in the news
—kidnapped/murdered—
must have suffered that evil

and why his mother must
anguish the loss of her child?

Does it comfort me to know
my Lord had suffered a greater
grief? I do not understand
so many things.

What good can come of tragedy?

A small rabbit scampers
carelessly under rolling tires.
Yet even scavengers seem to give
thanks as they fold their wings

over the still warm flesh. The trees
continue to wave their branches
in the wind and the earth doesn't sing
a eulogy. But no sparrow falls unnoticed.

        #

My eyes lift up
        the crimson light peels
               the clouds. Silhouettes
of herons recede, scissoring

horizon's edge ragged
        with a million butterflies, prayers
               nested in their wings.

The Man Who Saw the World

Alessandro Manzetti

The sherpas are afraid of the mountain
the mountain chews men and women
—they say—
it swallows them, slowly, into its narrow gullies
makes them slip, mashed
in its blue, honed intestine
then, suddenly
it raises its cold tongue, the avalanche
the icy acids of the end.

The sherpas tell many stories
about that mountain
they always look behind, they whisper
they are surrounded by ghosts
by men who have seen the world, before me
up there, on the top.

Nanga Parbat, a sleeping diamond
twenty-five thousand feet, twenty-five thousand carats
the fleas of my boots
their zig-zag on the large white whipped cream
the peak, between the traps of the crevasses
sharp ridges, green blood.
The Rupal wall, myself and nothing else.
—vertical glare—

The sherpas are under
they are singing, playing cards
while I'm filtering the oxygen and look for the devil up there, at the summit,
where I'm going to.
The sherpas say, making signs with their hands
that among those breaking rocks
lives the Beast.
—roars the Beast—
The Hell is above or below?

But now that I'm alone, with my alien mask
I can only hear the wind
the screaming of my muscles
the fingers disappeared
the slime that fills my lungs, drop by drop
the artic spice of illusion
becoming a flammable gas in my mouth.

Just a few feet, one hundred, two hundred
perhaps three hundred, even more.
I'll be on, on the rump of the Beast
maybe I'm experiencing an hallucination
because I see myself, next to me
exactly like me, but without boots
—without a shadow—
with all fingers in place.
He drags me up
he says that he wants to show me the world
I hold his glove, I follow *him*.

The white wall dissolves
I drag myself on the top.
The mountain laughs
it draws a red circle, where I have to go:
now I can see the world under there.
Something squeezes the clouds
freeing my view.
Shore of the Hell
a huge red lake, a giant bathtub
where my wife is floating, *my lost Venus*
along with many other bodies.
Another myself pushes me down
—an endless flight—
then the rope does its job:
my neck is broken
my feet dangling in the void.

It's done
my Venus emerges from the waters.
She stares at my eyes
I found her, right here
her face is no longer broken
the razor cuts of the disease are invisible
AIDS: that's what I pushed in her womb.
She hugs me
she walks slowly inside of me
melting the bones.
I've been waiting for this for two years.
"Let's go swimming in the red lake"

The cleaning lady will be soon
in my empty house.
She'll look at the urine stain on my pants
at my tongue hanging out
at my eyes turned towards the summit

she'll pull down my body
with disgust, with a dry smile.
Maybe she'll spit on my face
before calling the police.
She knows the whole story
—she hates me—
she will not lose the opportunity
to make me pay again.

The sherpas continue to play cards.
After the game is over, they come back to the valley
a long row of fleas, a coil of cold souls.
One of them looks back, for a moment
towards the summit.
He hears the laughter of the mountain
he thinks, before resuming the descent
that up there
another man has seen the world.

A Summoning of Monsters

Jack Hollis Marr

one: speaking

We had our tongues cut out
   when we were born.
They crafted others in their place:
his glass, hers bronze.
Mine was stone, sandpaper rough,
with a thread of hidden fire.

They did not like the stories the tongue they gave me told.

(His glass tongue chimes: his words are
beautiful and can break
so easily.
   You save your words when brittle-tongued
   fearing the silencing
shatter and crack.)

The tongue burned in my mouth, and I
swallowed stone-dust, the taste of
old dry clay, stale-crumbling.

I swallowed dust and gravel
digested, gizzard-churned

spat word on word
so acid that they crack my teeth
—and oh, the things I learned.

The dreadful things
I learned.

two: summoning

And now with my own tongue I call us come
soft-footed men and women
    with bronze tongues that speak rhyme,
who speak the sun:
monstrous, beautiful;
call It and Thing and That, marching in time.

(*Our name is Legion.*
We will eat you up.)

I call the scalpel-scar
call fistula, hypertrophy, adhesion, DVT
the tangle of hair growing in her cunt
the piss that leaks from the split-stitched base
of his prick.

I speak emergency rooms and midnight clinics
and call the turned-away:
stale blood on bandages, and I call
the black market and the grey
(mingle, you that mingle may).

I call
the hole that should not be
I call Lack
(these are *our* monsters)
(you)
I call
every scarred body
    (scared body)
every body

I call

the blunt nature-castrated mound
the hollowness within
voice of caverns and sinkholes:
(speak through me, oh my wound).

I call

our patched and monstrous flesh
that *will not die*
will not lie down
keeps moving
in spite of you
our hands that reach and teeth that gnaw
     (*will chew your bones*)
I call the thousand thousand years that we have been
despite your spite
I call our spite
our savage bitter spirit of revenge
that lives
in spite of you.

I.
call.
your.
fear.

I call the mirror we have been to you
cracked, now, from side to side:
Your slim protection. You must face
the monster now:
his tired face, still bruised,
and still
her burning eye,
so wide.

Concerning The Curious Burial Customs of the Witches of Megaira

Elizabeth R. McClellan

For A.F.S.B., friend of poets & fairy godparents, wise mother of witch-worlds

On Megaira the witches gave up
solstices and equinoxes fifty years
after the Displacement. The groves
(more shrubs than trees) flower
hydroponically, light-years from
the moon and seasons once
demanding such rites.

To be a witch,
wrote the elders of the time,
be practical. Make old ways new.

They circle still, under
strange-named moons:
dust-devil, star-bright,
snow and wolf and harvest
left to history.

The satellite shines into the groves, live,
streaming from unblinking camera towers
high above the unforgiving surface,
brushed clean by tiny automated processes.

Air and water the witches know. Fire
is an old recording that crackles
the blooms from the bottoms of ships
as they leave land, sky, atmosphere.

Earth? They live in drydust, even if
the young ones call the element
after their own planet, clunky
in the litany of air water fire,

favor goddesses of justice, truth, flowers,
beauty, underworlds, crossroads,
talk less and less of those who bless
rivers, oceans, trees, heavens, fertile ground.

Make old ways new, they say
to elders who grumble
as elders always will.

Planetary anthropologists of Earth's
diasporas delight in Megaira,
its strange traditions, emerging schisms
haunting phantoms of dollar signs, another
three-D witch-planet tell-all

(Tasteful. Educational, promoting
understanding, of course. *Ethical*—

We must always remember
what was done to these people.)

The death-customs alone, whisper
their greedy academic dreams.

Said the elder to the social scientist:

> *Our mothers knew we could not*
> *be buried in the earth of Megaira*
> *and return to the earth.*

> *Our sisters in Kemet*
> *bless Megaira's ground*
> *as Nepthys' body, for it mummifies*
> *without natron.*

> *The rest of us go to the earth*
> *we have, fertilize*
> *our tanks and farms,*
> *feed our families to come.*

> *It is grisly but it is our way.*
> *This planet was a punishment*
> *for sin we did not admit.*
> *We made old ways new,*
> *in peace, mostly.*

> *Who is envious and angry now,*
> *who torn apart for their crimes?*

Such wisdom is not the stuff of bestsellers.
Greed wins out. Thus the grainy film
that tore through intergalactic academe
like wildfire, better in its unblinking way
than a thousand artfully edited shock pieces,

the icon that got
so many bright graduate
student bodies searched
for hidden recorders,
secret allegiances,

by peoples who had never quite trusted
the nice-enough offworlders to start with.

EXTERIOR. NIGHT.

The witches gather around a rocket,
almost cartoonish, traditional old-Earth,
historical documentary-type. It towers
above the articulated figures,

white shifts over their suits.

There is the body of the dead witch,
wrapped in her winding sheet, no inch

of skin exposed, the dust gathering already
in the folds of her white shroud.

There is air to carry sound,
but unbreathable for lungs
evolved for less grit.
The film's focus is softened,
as if shot through a dirty cloud.

Helmet loudspeakers dulled with dust-patter
render the audio tinny, whispery,
properly arcane. It seems to be
the figure behind the corpse that speaks:

> *Why is this one*
> *not returned to the earth?*

One steps forward.

She must not be allowed the earth's strength.

> *Why may this one not feed*
> *those that come after?*

Another. *There is poison in her bones*
unfit for our children's marrow.

> *Why must this one be weak?*
> *What is her poison?*

A cacophony of voices. *She spoke lies,*
sent death and poverty, attacked the weak,
would not accept correction,
dared name herself queen.

> *Megaira has no queen, they say,*
> *in what seems like unison.*

Noted a well-respected
doctor of philosophy
and accidental film critic,
after the Megaira Incident:

> *the dead woman*
> *had been freeze-dried,*
> *her corpse preserved*
> *for an old-Earth year and a day—*
>
> *the elders circled*
> *every third night*
> *in the groves,*
> *one hundred twenty-two chances*

for anyone to come, speak,
conference in, claim her body

for their grove or garden
before the end. Some could have used
the nutrients. But none came.

This was not a puppet trial
but sentencing for a verdict
pronounced some time before
by pure consensus of silence.

An expensive punishment, too—
time was they went hungry
to pay for the parts, make sure
the next rocket lay ready.

They might go a hundred years
between launches.

Such wisdom is also not the stuff of bestsellers,
but produced respectable revenue, considering.

On the screen, a grim gavotte,
suited bodies bearing
the body, stiff between them,
solemnly sliding their burden
into the ship that will bear it.

One seals it, tiny torch a blinding spot
of light in the film, the others circling,
arms raised. The torch-bearer sears
indistinguishable sigils into the patch,
the door, continuing around the tube
as the circle hums protective harmonies.

It is not important,
said the good doctor,
if the door-seal survives
the path to the sun.

The real locking mechanism
would hold at seven gee,
though they have a lovely tale
of one whose bones fell
like a meteor shower, burning.

So cleansed by fire and air, they say,
Megaira forgave, blessed her bones.

They put meteors by the airlocks
in their homes, a new folk magic,
　　　long-ago apostate now
　　　fierce protector at the gate.

The dust whirls faster, erases the details.
Dim figures drop their arms, walk
counterclockwise three times, the welder
at the end of the line, filing

finally toward the hatch, the warrens,
leaving the towering ship
alone against the horizon line,
unmistakable, proud, silent.

A short delay,
then fire and noise , blossoming,
manifesting, pushing
rocket, body, sigils
skyward, sunward.

Demands

Mari Ness

1

He offers the gift with trembling hands.

2

She unwraps the silk with delicate teeth,
her lips brushing against what lies beneath.

3

Hidden within the silk's slippery strands:
two carefully forged shining silver hands,
precisely formed to a prince's demands.

4

Call to the skies,
　　　　call, my dear.
See if a savior
　　　　will appear.

5

The hands shimmer against the soft red silk.
A tender kiss falls on her salt laced skin.
      It is of the devil and all his ilk.
A tender kiss falls on her salt laced skin.
The hands shimmer against the soft red silk.

6

Once more, she is standing behind the mill,
the devil approaching as her savior,
the gold spilling out with its deathly chill.

The chalk. The circle. The grey dress she wore.
The air that had been so terribly still.
Her father's wet hands approaching once more.

7

A stumble. A slip.
A soft cry of pain.
Blood beads on her lower lip.
His hands tense with sudden strain.

So much he cannot say, explain.
So much left out of their courtship.
Hidden in silk, his scars remain.

8

Not words. Not silver. Not all of her tears—
Nothing—*nothing*—can truly keep her safe.
This is a truth she has known for long years.
Not words. Not silver. Not all of her tears.
She knows how hard silver weapons can chafe.
Even these hands, crafted against her fears.
Not words, not silver, not all of her tears—
Nothing. Nothing can truly keep her safe.

9

His mother, his *queen*. So noble, so sleek.
Promising to remove those heavy chains.
He should reach out, hold her, stroke her soft cheek.
Even broken, shattered, his love remains.

      I thought her an angel when we first met.

Good girls say nothing. Good girls do not shriek.
Her father, holding out those heavy chains.
She should reach out, hold him, touch his rough cheek.
Even broken, shattered, her love remains.

10

No need no need no need to fear
      Father, father. A cold tear
      falls hot on her bleeding arms.
      Father, father. So, so near—
The devil smiles at all her charms.

                    Sing, girl, sing.

Did you think you could make me disappear?
      She lifts up her handless arms.
      The devil giggles into her ear.

                    Sing, girl, sing.

11

The old axe had been blunted through hard use.
It took several blows. She still bears faint scars—
There, above the wrist. Where her sleeve is loose.
She once spent hours studying her skin,
the ragged stitches her own mouth had sewn,
watching her body, so painfully thin,
counting every single remaining bone,
flinching at everything that could have been:
a house of her own, with rough iron bars,
two hands that could swiftly knot a noose.
Not the distant hope of the silent stars.

12

In the garden that had been his retreat,
she once speared his precious pears with her tongue,
the juices on her chin so very sweet.
In the grey moonlight, she looked very young.

She once speared his precious pears with her tongue.
Not like the girls they had brought him to meet.
In the grey moonlight, she looked very young.
He found himself wanting to kiss her feet.

Not like the girls they had brought him to meet,
in the garden that had been his retreat.
He found himself wanting to kiss her feet.
The juices on her chin—so very sweet.

13

She summoned her demons to kill his own.
Just the demons, she said. *Just them alone.*
So she could refuse his hungry demands.
But the anger of demons—it expands.
It strengthened with each severed fingerbone.

They got some poison from the village crone.
Nothing that would kill. They promised her that.
She just wanted—*needed*—to make him well.
To make him the father she once had known.

It was hard, so hard. Her wrists had been sewn.
Still, she brought it to where her father sat.
It seemed so simple. Just a little spell.
To make him the father she once had known.

14

Good girls don't have demons. Good girls don't kill.
No matter what poisons their lives might bring.
Good girls do what their parents say they will.
Only good girls in stories wed the king.

She looks at the pain in his haunted eyes,
from a court glittering with treachery.
Her skin burns. She will not add her own lies.
No matter what his courtiers might see.

She kicks away his gift with two strong feet.
Raises the stumps of her disfigured wrists.
No silver will ever make those complete.
He will have to take her as she exists.

She watches to see if he understands.
He offers that gift with trembling hands.

The Memory-Thief

A. J. Odasso and Dominik Parisien

1.

The remembering is my Lethe
the cleansing of my crime
a trivialising of the theft;
but it is rare. There is much forgetting
and no great losses.
I am not as my vile siblings;
my love is the inconsequential:
an unremarkable kiss;
the flavour of a licked kindergarten chair;
the font on a wayside dinner menu;
an arrowhead of a word, sharp
as chipped obsidian, now magnificently dull.

The cortex is the center of loss
a manufacture of ideals and distortions
where I collect the lovely scraps.

2.

The thread on which I hang my heart
has worn thin. I'd love my betrayers
as bidden I've been, but forgiveness
wears thinner. I walk curb-stones
like tight-ropes, grasping at tendrils
of morning glory ghosts: this child
who crunched snail shells and lead
between her outstretched palms
has fled. Dogged, down alleys
I chase her; this voice, my mother
minding us—we collared strays
could only run so far. I learned
to shoot a bow and arrow, cut
both chain and buckle. We face
consequences now with something
resembling grace. And we pray—

O Memory, bless me. One brief
breath of smoke to the wind
is all I have been.

3.

There is a spectre of greater selfhood
gathering in the kleptomaniac
conglomeration of minutiae I keep:

>old buttons, black keys; words breathed
>too often fade in wonder; I wish for sleep
>to come as I speak, trail seeking fingers,
>dust till dawn (old sorrow, black dreams)

All thieves are porous; we know monoliths
are made of the miniscule and all things
comprised of a thousand thefts. We know minds
are the weakest of moorings for the *me*. And still
we steal, carry close invasive otherness, however
small. In the silence, we cannot but choose

>to fall down darkness to forgetting: once, I knew
>your every byway to the last worn stone
>and the heaviness your heart bore in lieu
>of heaviness hidden—we both loved best

the very tales we cannot have.

Ode to Yon Gliesan Orbs, or No?

Terrie Leigh Relf

After John Keats

You, still untrammeled just beyond our scopes?
You, 20,000 lightyears from our home,
dwarf of red yet giant within our hopes,
far beyond our own celestial dome.
What is it about you that draws us nigh?
Alien or human, we know not which
inhabitants you'll be, but we shall find
a way to fold time and space, make a stitch
and thus to join our planets by the bye,
sans starship, through the portals in our mind.

Gliese 581d, a rocky sphere,
with thirty days or so to fill a month?
581f? Further … hardly near.
667Cc? Light years? Dear,
'tis twenty-two and in Scorpio spins,

twenty-eight days to a month, and its size
four-times-plus-half our earth—just imagine …
Kepler 22b, we're nearly twins
with climes of 72; my passion
for this planet dares continue to rise.

HD 85512b, 'tis three-
plus-point-six times our earth and with such gales,
a mere thirty-five light years, then we're free!
Cast off—Unfurl those massive solar sails!
Or perhaps we'll journey to the frigid
surface of Gliese 581d, where
to enjoy seven times the space of earth.
'Tis possible our lives might be rigid,
unless some greenhouse gases
flourish there.
Let us join together, find a new berth!

I near forgot Gliese581c,
where light and heat, perhaps, are quite stable.
But let us pause to reflect on SETI,
to ask if communiqués are able
to reach us from these distances so vast.
Will our alien friends prefer to meet
us on their soil or ours, an orbital
station? Or do they watch us quite aghast,
concealed from radar just beyond our keep,
their systems on alert, nondigital?

Arctic oscillations have us frightened,
so much of earth is suffering from droughts;
our populace is hardly enlightened,
by the increasing radiation routes.
What are we to do? How will we journey
away from these annoying pessimists?
For I'm quite sure even as I stand here,
that we must ignore all these agonists.
Who is to judge this trans-stellar tourney,
when we leave this world … and just disappear?

Author's Note: This poem was inspired, in part, by Discovery.com article, "Gliese 581D: An Exoplanet Fit for Humans?" http://news.discovery.com/space/exoplanet-gliese-581d-human-habitation-110516.html

The Swooning

Mark Rich

Clare's slender fingers seek pitted prunes
from her fruit bowl marked by Celtic runes.
In her novel, knight fights, maiden swoons—

and an inner dawn threatens to break
into blinding glare, as if to make
light of this dim realm of the Awake.

Novel errs—a voice within tells her,
in Clare's own tones. Just now this murmur
stirs visions and scents of rose, fern, fir,

earth-mould underfoot in a dark wood ...
thoughts rise of promises felled, made good—
of day plunging to night, as it should.

Once she was other than what she has been
over these late years. Confused, boxed in,
she strains against a world grown thin

upon a trillion glowing screens,
lens-deep, that conceal by any means
human depths, render to shimmer-sheens

human heart-thoughts, and make pabulum
of news of nation, state and kingdom:
daily fare yields to daily boredom.

Self-styled Awakes have changed what was placed
in their care, for the worse. What once graced
self-aware life finds itself replaced

by low-denominator, low-cost
mockeries of a world now lost.
That journeyer, Human Culture, crossed

a flowing gold Styx and now arrives
at corporate gates where chastened lives,
finding welcome, crowd into vast hives

of compartmentalized moneybees
thriving on low wages and high fees.
Clare makes tea, sips. This dawning sense frees

old notions. (Awakes prefer new news,
not old, to back up considered views
factory-produced for all to use.)

She is thinking. A dim haze ascends
to wreathe her hair, aglow. Her mind tends
inward, mornings; and this novel sends

her into a life she had not known
as hers. She startles at a shriek, groan --
clang of steel! All that she calls her own

trembles, unbalanced, and falls: her maid
and knight, Gail-of-knives, falls beneath blade
thrust by landthief. In this bloodied glade

Clare, too, lies with face paled like white moon,
bleeding ... not in Victorian swoon
on fainting couch—velvet, dark maroon—

self-etherized in curtained parlor.
Not fashion-made but forced, her pallor:
she fades, she fails. Her lands, walls, manor—

her small wealth, modest accomplishments—
all bleed to soil. In her field-garments
the thieves bury her, while one comments

how she almost breathes. Yet she lies still
as they shovel. Chilled thoughts, stymied will,
emptied heart: what victors failed to kill

lingers quiescent in unmarked grave.
Not because clever—not because brave—
and not truly cleaving to life, save

in the way visions have of clinging
to shreds of hope ... streamers of dreaming ...
threads in strange designs that go spreading

wherever hearts put down roots and spread;
never quite alive, never quite dead;
never quite fleeing, never quite fled;

nowhere a steady flame, yet nowhere
wholly extinguished; not here, not there:
breathed in as woodsmoke, breathed out as air

to be shared—as words, as cries, as sighs—
she persists, awaiting waking eyes
that might glaze, recalling ancient skies.

Printed words before Clare smudged and shook,
while she dreamed this. She sets aside book
to dream more. Yet what the book mistook

for swoon was not after all a mistake:
for that which took maiden down would take
her down by any means that would make

others see her weakness. "She stands tall
but at feather-touch will swoon and fall."
Her slaying must mean nothing at all.

Who are these Awakes who seal shut gates
to dreams? Soul-harrowing toughs, ingrates,
landthieves—or ladies and lords of states

who regulate all scenes from behind?
We, the body; they the mind.
They, the designers; we, the designed.

Yet if she who died in bloody field
rises through souls when dreams come unsealed,
then even those rulers who boot-heeled

a globe to suit their group delusions
must once have breathed in what their minions
breathe out in morning dream-confusions—

must once have felt a touch not their own
from within, from fingers that have grown
far-reaching, there beneath soil and stone.

Even if their schoolings damped and quelled
a youthful sense that never rebelled
into outer life, they still once held

emanations within their beings ...
reverberations ... echoed beatings
of a stilled heart ... murmuring breathings.

Yet those who command by wealth and laws
and social pressures have named their cause
the Awakening. Capital draws

veils away: their single truth must stand
nakedly. In a world well planned
veils, scarves and dresses have all been banned

to make other truths shrink in cash-cold.
Arts matter? Yes—when arts that are sold
are mass-produced. Children must be told

not to invent, but to dissemble
emotions; factories assemble
musical kits to render simple

the mass-dronings that predominate
among songs we sing, hum, imitate,
and call our own. People must placate

inner demons with such mass fodder,
and satiate artistic hunger
by such means of heeling it under.

Books must have blood, death, titillation,
and mirrors for self-satisfaction,
or else myths of self-elevation—

anything to make readers forget
their morning alarm clocks have been set
by needs not of their selfhoods, but debt.

What if, Clare muses, only dreamers
are awake, and all Awakes, sleepers?
In fake freedom from mental slumbers

they move, wide-eyed, remotely controlled
by cash flows, their actions bought and sold
from a distance—drones of the bankrolled.

Yet what can she do? Surely not yield
yet again to the over-well-heeled
now that she knows that in bloodied field

her soul once swooned into her own gore—
that she died—that on Stygian shore
she faded, becoming less, then more

than what she was. A spark of wisdom—
or hope of spark—chaotic, random,
fire-bright! A clear note, a Clare hum—

back of her throat wanting out, or in!
Consequential noise, meaningful din,
bated confusion too long held in—

verging on incandescence, verging
on madness, leaving her crushed, weeping,
collapsing—as her blood starts singing!

Principles of Entropy

Shelagh Rowan-Legg

I

press your ear against
the Egyptian cotton sheet
you will hear the universe
gravitating towards expansion

each of the thousand threads
straining against this
forced dissipation

let your head lie across
your lover's chest
the universe will pull him away
in its own time

II

each cell of the body
is Schrödinger's cat
unaware of its fate
they crowd against each other
as bodies in rush hour subways
hot and tired and anxious

III

five trillion atoms
could fit on the head of a pin
so I take a small knife
and divide my heart
into as many pieces
to refit into a newer
smaller space

IV

it is
impossible
to determine
simultaneously both
position

and movement
with certainty

not the waves of the ocean but the waves of space
not suitable for drowning but for carrying
into the flat velvet black
you are crushed and each part of your body touches the other
toes against elbows back against knees

V

the bird pecks his beak
against
the flat velvet black
mistake it
for a sheet of seeds
particles fall
unaware
of wind
stripping them
still
bit
by
bit
into
essentiality and
insignificance

VI

keep a record
of the swings of a pendulum
the timing of each swoosh
will decide everything

future is determined
by hands that reach
between each tick
reach the wrong time
and they return empty
thirty-two million swings too late

Eolian Conscientia

Mary Turzillo & Marge Simon

The song at midnight
began soft, beseeching,
but burningly sweet, as if from some other star.

pianissimo melody
the moon flickering through clouds
sunlight on a child's hair

The volume so low at first
the people thought it a hymn in their heads
something each had heard long ago,
that song that makes you first realize
that all things die eventually,
that you will therefore die,
but because of the brave music,
death is right, it is fine.

dedicated moments
homages to dead heroes
a canticle, a requiem, a dirge

Not human voices, but canny, wise even.
And the song grew louder
as the chorus swelled
joined by sea creatures, bats, blind frogs,
insects with human eyes, and yes, angels,

accelerando accompanied by Bosch
a world of dreams and nightmares,
as forms flicker and change within notes

angels with throats made of molten metal.
Their harmonies drilled into human ears,
a wire strung too tight,
black noise behind telephone silence, except
louder and loudest,
and people tried to make out the words.
Some began to preach the words

that apes could sing hosannas

but they were just sounds,
there was no sense to them
just the smothering membrane of song,
a cloud too loud to be music

more like jet engines
pelting, irradiating, throbbing,
as it drove even old men mad,

and mere humans lay on the ground
twisting to escape the music, or maybe to join it,
to get inside it, to let it inside them,
though it screamed, it burned,
like electricity in your forehead exploding forever,

gaining forte, volcanic
as a revolution of exponentials,
a demonic ensemble

and then it crescendoed:
sforzando.
Ears bled, eyes shriveled, song seized tongues,
and all men and women joined the chorus
the chorus coaxing death, insisting.
Except me
except me and some others
deaf from birth.

the lucky ones,
lacking tympani

We had felt the thrumming
had seen the folk convulsing on ballroom floors.
Fear drew us together

clutching at phantoms of an unholy opera
we were not privy to attend

Now we are left
and nobody can describe the song
but we must bury those bodies

anointed with death's perfume

and hope that the song does not get in our heads
though I begin to hear it
even as my wife described it
talking with her quick fingers.

beyond the cochlea's fluid,
Munch knew it as a scream
in blood red clouds

I run to the caves
which will not hide me

Let the Fire Decide

Sarah Wright

"We want to dance!"
Said orange and red,
"Anytime we get the chance,
We dance, and dance, and dance, and ..."

White and blue sunk and sighed.
The wise ones, pale, thin and hot,
Were used to being pushed aside,
By the vaudeville show living on top.

Yellow pulled back,
Mulling it over,
Always last,
Thick and hot—
From in-between,
The base beneath the fire's blast.

The fire was lit for fairy tales,
Behind the local mega church.
Around the front, a child wailed,
As Brothers Grimm was ripped away.

"Who cares?" said red.
"For fire to dance, it needs to be fed!"

"You should care, you crazy beast,
You'd turn a Library into your feast."
That was blue piping in,
Then it disappeared and came back again.

White hissed, black smoke was forlorn,
Orange writhed its serpentine form,
It never cared once red was born.
Yellow couldn't really decide,
Either burn fairy tales or prepare to die.

White and blue already said nay,
Orange was for it, as red said yay.
That left the black, wispy carbon remains,
That spun off the top and always complained.
It was always yellow who had to decide,
To burn things up or refuse to light.

Should we stab the lore with a Baptist stake?
Yellow thought to itself amidst internal debate.

Before the pile of fantasy books,
The preacher preached and the children were hooked.
Men came to the fire with torches unlit,
But yellow pulled back and that was it.

Red shrank and screamed in bloody protest,
Orange beneath shut up and acquiesced.
Said blue and white with a sigh of relief,
"Good call on that one.
That's why you're the chief."

Once the fire had put itself out,
The men couldn't figure what that was about.
It wasn't raining and plenty of air,
But for years to come no fire would burn there.

Conservation of Energy

Alvaro Zinos-Amaro

Proposition:
Hating the world
is strictly logical
when your loved one is
dying.

Proof:
You watch her neurons choke
You watch holes inside her brain grow
like blackened maws from another dimension
—oh, what endlessly wasteful multiverse!—
you watch as her brain itself shrinks
disease–riddled (or, better said, disease–irresolved
since there's no solution to this particular puzzle)
convolutions de–convoluting
speech bubbling over into babbling
memories of how to "sit down" or "swallow"
being sat down upon and swallowed
by creeping entropy.

And you understand that each iota of her death
is nothing but diminished energy,
a loss of information,
and these things—energy and information—
you are painfully aware
must be conserved

tyrannical natural law
and so as your loved one *dies*
the world *lives* a little more
and everyone around you
and the trees and flowers
and even the lakes and mountains and red giants and white dwarfs
and the quantum space–time foam
and that neighbor who's always smoking
leery, dangling cigarette and stained wife–beater, the one who lingers and
doesn't smile when you pick up your mail,
they all glow a little brighter
they hold hands without even knowing it,
infinitesimally enriched,
unwitting beneficiaries of her
disintegration.

And so you *hate* them,
you pulse with venom for them,
for how ignorant they are
regarding their own provenance,
for how they remind you
of what you no longer have
and of what they have gained—unwantingly, unknowingly—
instead.

Quantitative Implications:
You remember in time
that you too
have been enriched
by this death. By countless deaths. The elements in your body
are particles of a melody
sung by Shiva
in exploding stars
and so you do the only natural thing.

You abandon discrimination
you relent in your binary thinking
of me–versus–them
and you learn to hate *yourself*

with abandon and perhaps glee,
without pretense,
you are now one as them.

Unabashedly imploding
to offset all those explosions
that led
to you.

1978	Long	Gene Wolfe	"The Computer Iterates the Greater Trumps"
	Short	Duane Ackerson	"The Starman"
	(tie)	Sonya Dorman	"Corruption of Metals"
		Andrew Joron	"Asleep in the Arms of Mother Night"
1979	Long	Michael Bishop	"For the Lady of a Physicist"
	Short	Duane Ackerson	"Fatalities"
	(tie)	Steve Eng	"Storybooks and Treasure Maps"
1980	Long	Andrew Joron	"The Sonic Flowerfall of Primes"
	Short	Robert Frazier	"Encased in the Amber of Eternity"
	(tie)	Peter Payack	"The Migration of Darkness"
1981	Long	Thomas M. Disch	"On Science Fiction"
	Short	Ken Duffin	"Meeting Place"
1982	Long	Ursula K. Le Guin	"The Well of Baln"
	Short	Raymond DiZazzo	"On the Speed of Sight"
1983	Long	Adam Cornford	"Your Time and You: A Neoprole's Dating Guide"
	Short	Alan P. Lightman	"In Computers"
1984	Long	Joe Haldeman	"Saul's Death: Two Sestinas"
	Short	Helen Ehrlich	"Two Sonnets"
1985	Long	Siv Cedering	"Letter from Caroline Herschel (1750–1848)"
	Short	Bruce Boston	"For Spacers Snarled in the Hair of Comets"
1986	Long	Andrew Joron	"Shipwrecked on Destiny Five"
	Short	Susan Palwick	"The Neighbor's Wife"
1987	Long	W. Gregory Stewart	"Daedalus"
	Short	Jonathan V. Post	"Before the Big Bang: News from the Hubble Large Space Telescope"
	(tie)	John Calvin Rezmerski	"A Dream of Heredity"
1988	Long	Lucius Shepard	"White Trains"
	Short	Bruce Boston	"The Nightmare Collector"
	(tie)	Suzette Haden Elgin	"Rocky Road to Hoe"
1989	Long	Bruce Boston	"In the Darkened Hours"
	(tie)	John M. Ford	"Winter Solstice, Camelot Station"
	Short	Robert Frazier	"Salinity"

1990	Long	Patrick McKinnon	"dear spacemen"
	Short	G. Sutton Breiding	"Epitaph for Dreams"
1991	Long	David Memmott	"The Aging Cryonicist in the Arms of His Mistress Contemplates the Survival of the Species While the Phoenix Is Consumed by Fire"
	Short	Joe Haldeman	"Eighteen Years Old, October Eleventh"
1992	Long	W. Gregory Stewart	"the button and what you know"
	Short	David Lunde	"Song of the Martian Cricket"
1993	Long	William J. Daciuk	"To Be from Earth"
	Short	Jane Yolen	"Will"
1994	Long	W. Gregory Stewart and Robert Frazier	"Basement Flats: Redefining the Burgess Shale"
	Short	Bruce Boston	"Spacer's Compass"
	(tie)	Jeff VanderMeer	"Flight Is for Those Who Have Not Yet Crossed Over"
1995	Long	David Lunde	"Pilot, Pilot"
	Short	Dan Raphael	"Skin of Glass"
1996	Long	Margaret B. Simon	"Variants of the Obsolete"
	Short	Bruce Boston	"Future Present: A Lesson in Expectation"
1997	Long	Terry A. Garey	"Spotting UFOs While Canning Tomatoes"
	Short	W. Gregory Stewart	"Day Omega"
1998	Long	Laurel Winter	"why goldfish shouldn't use power tools"
	Short	John Grey	"Explaining Frankenstein to His Mother"
1999	Long	Bruce Boston	"Confessions of a Body Thief"
	Short	Laurel Winter	"egg horror poem"
2000	Long	Geoffrey A. Landis	"Christmas (after we all get time machines)"
	Short	Rebecca Marjesdatter	"Grimoire"
2001	Long	Joe Haldeman	"January Fires"
	Short	Bruce Boston	"My Wife Returns as She Would Have It"
2002	Long	Lawrence Schimel	"How to Make a Human"
	Short	William John Watkins	"We Die as Angels"

2003	Long	Charles Saplak and Mike Allen	"Epochs in Exile: A Fantasy Trilogy"
	(tie)	Sonya Taaffe	"Matlacihuatl's Gift"
	Short	Ruth Berman	"Potherb Gardening"
2004	Long	Theodora Goss	"Octavia Is Lost in the Hall of Masks"
	Short	Roger Dutcher	"Just Distance"
2005	Long	Tim Pratt	"Soul Searching"
	Short	Greg Beatty	"No Ruined Lunar City"
2006	Long	Kendall Evans and David C. Kopaska-Merkel	"The Tin Men"
	Short	Mike Allen	"The Strip Search"
2007	Long	Mike Allen	"The Journey to Kailash"
	Short	Rich Ristow	"The Graven Idol's Godheart"
2008	Long	Catherynne M. Valente	"The Seven Devils of Central California"
	Short	F.J. Bergmann	"Eating Light"
2009	Long	Geoffrey A. Landis	"Search"
	Short	Amal El-Mohtar	"Song for an Ancient City"
2010	Long	Kendall Evans and Samantha Henderson	"In the Astronaut Asylum"
	Short	Ann K. Schwader	"To Theia"
2011	Long	C.S.E. Cooney	"The Sea King's Second Bride"
	Short	Amal El-Mohtar	"Peach-Creamed Honey"
2012	Long	Megan Arkenberg	"The Curator Speaks in the Department of Dead Languages"
	Short	Shira Lipkin	"The Library, After"
2013	Long	Andrew Robbert Sutton	"Into Flight"
	Short	Terry Garey	"The Cat Star"
2014	Long	Mary Soon Lee	"Interregnum"
	Short	Amal El-Mohtar	"Turning the Leaves"

For a complete list of past Rhysling winners, runners-up, and nominees, see the SFPA Fhysling archive at **sfpoetry.com/ra/rhysarchive.html.**

1999	Bruce Boston
2005	Robert Frazier
2008	Ray Bradbury
2010	Jane Yolen

A SFPA Grand Master designation may be conferred by the SFPA President with consensus of the membership to an individual living at the time of selection whose body of work shall reflect the highest artistic goals of the SFPA, who shall have been actively publishing within speculative poetry for a period of no fewer than 20 years, and whose poetry has been noted to be exceptional in merit, scope, vision and innovation.

For further information, see **sfpoetry.com/grandmasters.html**

HOW TO JOIN SFPA

SFPA members receive *Star∗Line*, the quarterly journal of the Science Fiction Poetry Association, filled with poetry, reviews, articles, and more. Members also receive the annual *Rhysling Anthology*, containing the best SF/F/H poetry of the previous year (selected by the membership), and *Dwarf Stars*, an edited anthology of the best short-short speculative poetry of the previous year.

Each member may nominate one short poem and one long poem for the *Rhysling Anthology* and then vote for the Rhysling Awards from the anthology. Members may nominate poems of ten lines or fewer to the *Dwarf Stars* editor and vote for that award as well. SFPA also sponsors the Elgin Awards for speculative poetry chapbooks and full-length books, and an annual poetry contest.

SFPA Membership – One Year
$15 • PDF only for *Star∗Line, Dwarf Stars, Rhysling Anthology*
$30.00 • United States
$35.00 • Canada/Mexico
$40.00 • Overseas

Five Years
$60 • PDF only
$120 • United States
$140 • Canada/Mexico
$160 • Overseas

Lifetime
Payable in three payments over a period of three years.
$200 • PDF only
$450 • United States
$500 • Canada/Mexico
$550 • Overseas
(Failure to make all payments reverts membership to the number of years equivalent to the amount actually paid.)

All prices are in U.S. funds. Checks and money orders should be made out to the Science Fiction Poetry Association and sent to:

SFPA Treasurer
P.O. Box 907
Winchester, CA 92596

or pay online via PayPal to SFPATreasurer@gmail.com.

www.ingramcontent.com/pod-product-compliance
Lightning Source LLC
LaVergne TN
LVHW051636080426

835511LV00016B/2356